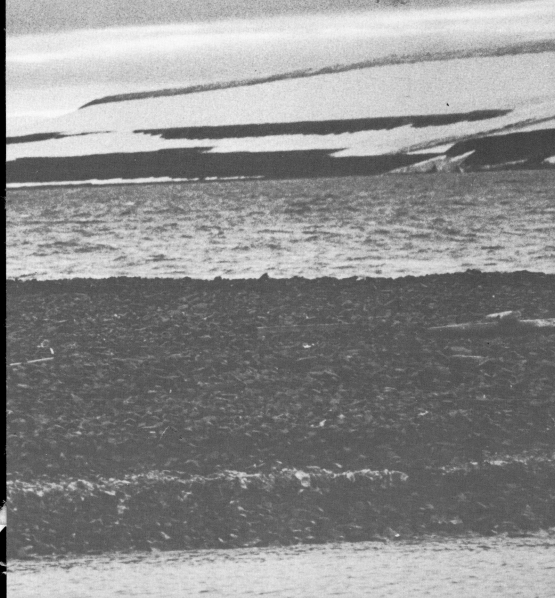

THE YEAR OF THE POLAR BEAR

THE YEAR
OF THE
POLAR BEAR

by

Thomas J. Koch

THE BOBBS-MERRILL COMPANY, INC.
INDIANAPOLIS   NEW YORK

I am indebted to Betty Diersen for her early encouragement and to Patricia Coffin for her translation of Eskimo terms. I would particularly like to thank my wife, Laurie, for her readings and suggestions.

To my Mother and Father

CONTENTS

THE YEAR OF THE POLAR BEAR

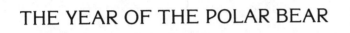

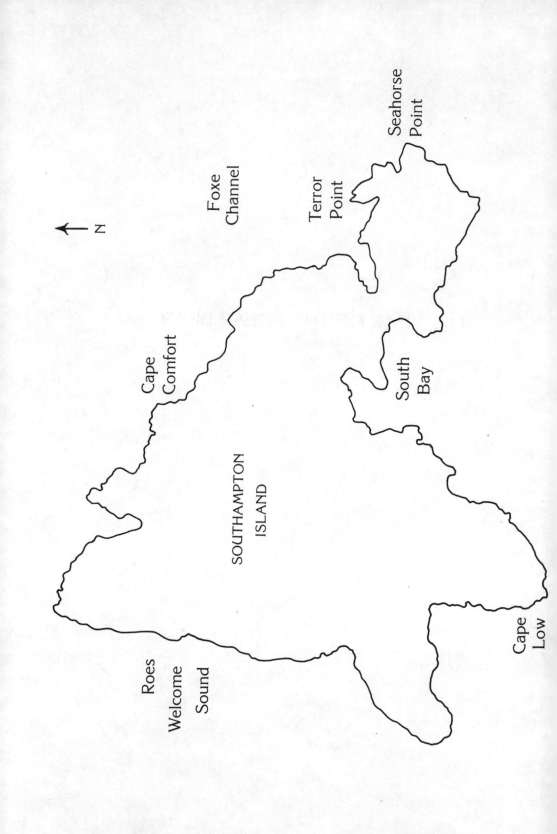

DECEMBER
SIKO—The Season
of Ice Solid Winter

It is the beginning of December. The mother delivers herself of a tiny male cub. She gently but firmly nudges him from the fetal sleep that has been his existence for eight months. The warmth and protection of the womb are no longer his, and he feels the cold. Only a hundred miles from the Arctic Circle, he shivers convulsively. A second cub is born—a sister to the first. Both pant and puff. Each breath in the Arctic winter is a cold struggle.

If Little Cub could see, he would find himself locked in a snowy cocoon, a polar bear den. With their only connection to the outside world a small air vent, the bear family lives beneath the surface of the snow. The sun is just above the horizon, and the vent admits only a trace of light. All that is visible is the dark shadow of the quietly sleeping bear.

Today Little Cub, his sister, and his mother will begin a social relationship that will last for a year and a half. Solitary animals, except during the mating season, during the rearing of cubs, or during unusual feeding circumstances, polar bears rarely live communally. Combatant by nature, they find such individualism protective. Anyone witnessing a fight between two 1000-pound he-bears would be convinced that solitude was the most practical life style for them to follow.

Outside their den the polar night is growing longer and darker. Even though it is midmorning, the sun has just made its appearance. Once dawn has arrived, it will quickly turn to night again before midafternoon. Even at noon it seems that at any moment the sun will set. The snow is faintly orange, reflecting the color of the sky. Long blue shadows accent the slightest knobs and hillocks.

Foremost in the Arctic is the cold—the dead, cold winter. The ground freezes so hard that it splits with a loud crack. Leads of open water appear hazy with steam. Wind howls and snow grinds. There is little that survives each winter except the cold itself.

Down the northeast coast of the island called Shugliak by the Eskimos, wisps of steam mark a polar bear denning haven. The cubbing season is at its peak. The mysteries of birth and life are slowly revealed, just as they have been inside Little Cub's den.

Now that Little Cub has been licked clean and dry by his mother, he clings to her for warmth. Even though the temperature in the den is forty degrees warmer than outside, it is still below freezing. The layers of snow between the bears and the outside air help to insulate them from the worst weather, but it is still cold.

Little Cub at birth weighs a mere pound, one-seven-hundredth of his mother's weight. This pound is spread over an eight-inch-long body. When curled up as he was in his mother's womb, he is the same size as the stick of butter in the compartment in a refrigerator door.

Little Cub, being born so small, is at a great disadvantage. It is a well-known fact that the greater one's body volume, the easier it is to conserve heat. Fortunately his mother keeps him warm.

Little Cub has yet to be well defined as a polar bear. His unpigmented body is barely covered with short, thin hair. He could probably be smuggled into a number of other animal maternity chambers without immediate discovery.

Except for his curved, razor-sharp claws, used to hold his mother's breast, Little Cub is totally dependent on her help. He was born blind, and his eyes are still closed. Unable to hear, he must wait four weeks for his auditory passages to grow open. It will be more than two months before Little Cub's sense of smell —the most important sense of all in his life—will develop enough for him to sniff out his surroundings.

When Little Cub's mother awoke from her deep winter sleep, she delivered the infants and then gave them care. As soon as the cubs were born, she lifted them to her breast and leaned against the den wall. Since the day was cold, she breathed over them, warming their chilled bodies. On particularly frigid days the mother must reach the den's air vent and pack it with snow to prevent the warm air from escaping. During the first month the female will hold a constant vigil to keep the naked cubs from the den's frozen floor and certain death.

Little Cub's mother uses her oversize paw to position the cubs near her nipples. Both cubs, clinging to their mother, begin sucking. They will spend every moment in the first week of their life at the breast, sucking the thick milk and sleeping.

During the four-month wait inside his den, Little Cub will suckle six times each day. He will spend progressively less time as he grows older and becomes more proficient. After temporarily drying one breast, he will quickly switch to the other. Once he and his sister are satisfied by their mother's four teats, they will quickly fall asleep.

Polar bear milk has the appearance and consistency of condensed milk, with a fishy odor. The composition of polar bear milk reflects the animal's high-fat dietary requirements.

Thirty per cent of the milk is fat, whereas the milk we drink contains only 4 per cent fat. The cubs receive almost the same amounts of protein and lactose from their milk as do their young cousins, the seal, the porpoise, and the whale.

The history of man's knowledge of the polar bear can be traced back as early as nineteen hundred years ago. In the year 57 Calpurnius wrote of seeing white bears set against seals. Traditionally, many cultures decreed that manhood was not achieved until a polar bear was killed with the hunter's spear. Japanese imperial records note that in the year 658 polar bears were sighted by the inhabitants of both Japan and Manchuria. Norwegian voyagers, during the ninth, tenth, and eleventh centuries, encountered the polar bear while traveling in northern Russia and Greenland. Later, in the twelfth and thirteenth centuries, Arabian merchants in northern Russia were able to trade for the magnificent white hides. We can only imagine what treasures Arabian princes paid to have these splendid pelts adorn their homes. Marco Polo, at approximately the same time, reported seeing the white bears among the Tartar nomads in his travels in northern Asia. In Scandinavia polar bear skins were used to warm priest's feet as they celebrated Mass. Men in search of favor gave live polar bears to their kings.

Our earliest recorded reference from North America was made less than one hundred years after Columbus discovered America. In 1585 John Davis sailed into Cumberland Sound on the southeast coast of Baffin Island and observed: "So soone as we were come to an anker in Totnes Rode under mount Raleigh we espied four white beares at the foote of the mount. We, supposing them to bee goates or wolves, manned our boats, and went toward them: but when wee came neere the shore, wee found them to be white beares of a monstruous bignesse."

Late in December the current from the north slowly brings the ice floes and a pregnant she-bear to the ice-locked shores of Shugliak. The female slips off the floe and swims the last few yards to shore. Her disembarkation is accompanied by a shower of water from her white coat. Pulses of pain drive her down to her side. In an aberration of her biological time clock, her cub is born. Miles from a suitable denning site, she faces a dilemma. She knows her already low fat reserves will not sustain her through the demanding suckling period. Without shelter, the windblown cold will slowly penetrate her and the cub. The need to survive overrides her confused maternal instincts, and she walks away to find food. The cub quickly dies.

Unencumbered by maternal instinct Little Cub's father is still moving on the ice pack. The he-bear is hunting for his favorite food, the seal, trying to build up layers of fat to last the winter. In a single day he wanders great distances, often climbing pressure ridges to view the vast expanses of ice. When there are no ridges, he will stand up on his hind legs, searching the area with his eyes and also carefully trying to catch the musky odor of the seal with his nose. With the polar night at its height, the lack of light makes the task more difficult than usual.

Little Cub's father, like most other male polar bears, will remain outside the walls of a sheltering den for much of the winter, moving abroad even when temperatures drop as low as 65 degrees below zero Fahrenheit. Particularly during winter months when seals are difficult to locate, male polar bears are known to travel great distances—so far, in fact, that the hair is worn off the soles of their feet.

During the long, dark night of the polar winter, Vilhjalmur Stefansson wrote:

> I had just killed a seal and secured it when over my shoulder I saw three bears approaching. It was past the twilight noon, and their yellowish-white outlines against the pure white ice were so indistinct that they could not be seen except when they were moving, or at

least their bodies could not, except for the shiny black noses. When bears are on the alert, and when they either see something indistinctly, or are expecting to see something the presence of which they suspect, they move their necks and their white bodies to peer about in a peculiar snaky way. These particular bears made themselves conspicuous now and then by standing on their hind legs, which brought their profiles against the sky.

In open spaces when the weather is cold, a polar bear, male or female, is capable of outrunning a team of huskies over distances as long as seven miles. Even if the ice is rough, speeds of twenty to twenty-five miles per hour are reached over short distances. While being pursued by huskies or man, polar bears tend to avoid land and to favor leads of open water and ice floes.

If confronted with ridges of ice, the bear can easily jump over six-foot-high barriers. Once upon a ridge of ice, he can easily jump down from walls more than ten feet high. When it is impossible to leap over barriers, he can scale faces of sheer ice or snow by digging his claws into the small cracks or crevices. On steep, icy slopes the bear will ski, using his front feet to glide to the bottom.

If one watches a polar bear traveling on ice, it will be noticed that he takes a sinuous route to avoid walking through puddles of water. In many of the puddles, sharp ice needles, standing on end, can be painful if stepped on. Thin frozen ice is also avoided—the polar bear is afraid of falling through.

With his long, thick hair and padding of blubber, the polar bear appears to be clumsy and uncoordinated. In reality, however, he is agile in capturing his prey and moving across the hazardous ice fields.

John Muir, the naturalist, spent much of his life crusading for the preservation of our earth's natural beauty. Writing of his mystical relation to nature's wonders, he struggled to make America wilderness-conscious. In his journal written in 1881, he described the polar bear as he viewed the animal on the cruise of the *Corwin,* a ship sailing in Arctic waters.

> . . . he is a noble-looking animal and of enormous strength, living bravely and warm amid eternal ice. They certainly do not seem to have been fed upon lately to any marked extent, for we found them everywhere in abundance along the edge of the ice, and they appeared to be very fat and prosperous, and very much at home, as if the country had belonged to them always. They are the unrivaled master-existences of this icebound solitude. . .

The range of the polar bear extends across five circumpolar countries: Canada, Denmark (Greenland), Norway (Svalbard), the U.S.A. (Alaska), and the U.S.S.R. It may be said that there are two factors controlling the polar bear's range: seals and ice. If the ice does not break up every summer, the seals will not have the open water they require. Without seals to hunt, the polar bear must move to more productive and life-sustaining feeding grounds.

Stefansson described the interaction he found in Alaska and Canada:

> If the coast is open as in northern Alaska, you can go five or ten miles to seaward and find a place where the wind has broken the ice and where the cakes are in motion. Here you will find seals swimming about in the water like bathers in a pond, and the tracks of polar bears that live on the seals may meet you anywhere. But in places like Coronation Gulf there is land on every side, and the ice does not move from November, when it forms, until the following June or July, when it breaks up some two months after summer and green grass have come upon all the surrounding lands. There are no polar bear tracks on this ice except in rare years.

Meteorologists studying weather charts and statistics from the early 1900's to the present have predicted a warming of the polar regions. This trend that is expected to crest in two hundred years will seriously reduce the polar bear's range due to the decreasing area covered by the ice pack. If there is an increase of open water, navigators would be able to weave through both the American and Soviet Arctic. With ships contaminating the water with oil and foul-smelling garbage, the polar bear would be further contained.

Little Cub has grown quickly in his first month. After his frequent nursing his body is covered with thick, woolly fur. His white coat has blunted some of the cold that shocked him the day he was dropped from his mother's 102-degree womb. The naked nose, lips, and foot pads are slowly being shaded. His birth wrinkles are disappearing with each new pound. Now he begins to look like a polar bear cub.

JANUARY
AKJUK—The Season
of Short Days

The Eskimos who inhabit the island call it Shugliak—the island-pup that is suckling the continent mother-dog. Known to our culture as Southampton Island, the home of Little Cub looms like a sentry at the mouth of Hudson Bay.

If we started a survey of the island from the western shore, where the waters of Roes Welcome Sound glide by, we would find seemingly endless miles of Arctic tundra. The tundra gradually rises to the eastern coast with its high, granite cliffs. Departing from Seahorse Point, the eastern coast's southern tip, we would find a very rough and rugged shoreline. Cliffs standing three hundred feet tall guard the invading fjords and river valleys.

What makes this nineteen-thousand-square-mile desolate heap of rock look like a hospitable denning haven to polar bears year after year? If we crawled up one of the many rocky river beds on the eastern coast, we would find well-protected refuges where snow has accumulated from the blizzards rolling across the tundra. Polar bears seek these insulated drifts in which to

9

overwinter and bring forth their cubs. Without a secluded birth chamber, the polar bear cubs' chances of survival would be seriously reduced.

Outside Little Cub's den it is an unusual night. A peculiar spectacle, rarely seen, moves across the sky. The northern lights, nature's psychedelic blaze of color, undulate across the sky. Like a towering waterfall cascading from the sky, the lights slowly wind their way down.

The winter solstice has just passed, and the sun will not warm Shugliak for some time. After days of terrifying storms the night is clear. The temperature drops—40, 50, 60 degrees below zero. Little Cub and his sister awake from their sleep. Aware of the fall in temperature, they begin to whimper. Their cries stir the maternal instinct deep in their mother, waking her from her winter sleep. She responds by curling up tightly, her forepaws holding her hind paws, pressing Little Cub and his sister tightly to her breast. Once again she breathes over them to ease the effects of the deep cold.

Little Cub, now growing rapidly, has opened his eyes for the first time. The den is too dark to see his mother or sister—it really makes no difference, since his eye muscles will have to strengthen before they can focus. By the time he emerges from the den, his vision will be as good as his mother's.

Once the bitter cold moves past their island, Little Cub tries to crawl for the first time. He digs into his mother's thick coat, attempting to find a good hold. Slowly he moves a few inches. Pleased at his newfound mobility, he blindly travels over his mother's sizable body. Without warning, Little Cub falls to the frozen floor. Stunned by the freezing cold, he cries for help. His mother sweeps him back to her body. She knows that from now on her cub will demand much attention.

The cubs' mother sits on her rump and leans against the wall of the den. With both cubs eager to suckle, she places them between her hind legs and with her large forepaw holds them to her breast. The cubs attack the nipples, sucking the rich milk.

The nursing cubs, even though quite proficient, are very noisy. Occasionally the nipples will slip from their mouths, and slurps will rapidly change to whimpers. Once they are redirected, they are back sucking the warm milk. Periodically a drop of milk forms on the cubs' lips and drops to the floor of the den—there to stay frozen until next summer.

A few miles down the coast, a cousin of Little Cub is also learning to crawl in his den. The little white bear moves down his mother's side. The mother bear has gone into a deep winter sleep. Without warning, the great she-bear suddenly moves. The little bear slips off and falls between her and the wall of the den. Like a great barrel, the mother rolls against the wall. With all his wind squeezed out, the cub is unable even to whimper. He is quickly suffocated and crushed to death. Soon her heavy breasts, filled with milk, will wake her to the sad sight of her dead cub.

Little Cub's father has covered many miles, searching for seals. Now that the severest winter weather is thrashing the Arctic, the polar seas are freezing up and polar bears have a difficult time finding the seal breathing holes. Once a seal's breathing hole or "aglos," as the Eskimos term it, is found, long hours of waiting are demanded if a seal is to be captured. More often than not, Little Cub's father is hungry.

Since early in the day, light snow has been falling. Little Cub's father, ignoring the storm, has continued his hunt. As the day progresses, the wind blows harder and the storm turns into a violent blizzard. Able to see only a few feet in front of his muzzle, he can no longer hunt. On a small, protected pile of snow Little Cub's father pivots again and again on his hind legs, carving a shallow pit. He curls up tightly in it and hides his nose between his paws. Allowing the snow to cover him, he sleeps off the winter storm.

Most zoologists flinch when the word "hibernate" is spoken or written. Once this word has been mentioned, the educated listener usually demands a definition of terms and a family-by-family discussion of what type of sleep behavior an individual group displays. Even in many modern zoology textbooks used today, confusion has not been cleared up. Polar bears and, for that matter, the other members of the bear family do not hibernate.

Polar bears exhibit "carnivorean lethargy." This particular sleep behavior can be characterized as a deep sleep which enables them to escape extended periods of poor hunting and extreme weather conditions, and to bring forth and nurture cubs in a protected maternity den as Little Cub's mother is doing. Once the bear has entered this deep sleep, various body functions slow down or are completely stopped. Metabolism, the creation and use of energy, in a resting bear is much slower than usual. The body temperature drops one or two degrees from normal. With minimal activity, the oxygen demand is much lower than usual. As a result the respiration or breathing rate is slowed down, just as in human sleep. Since no food is being consumed, the digestive organs and kidneys cease functioning almost completely.

The question comes to mind—how can the bear last the whole winter without food? Before Little Cub's mother entered her den, she spent many days hunting and building up her fat reserves. When she did enter the den, a layer of fat, more than three inches thick in some parts, covered most of her body. Now the fat is being used as her source of energy, sustaining her over the winter and also insulating her from the cold.

Zoologists have found that before polar bears enter their dens, they block their anal passages with earth, grasses, moss, and even their own hair. This prevents them from soiling the den and eventually themselves during the long winter. When Little Cub's mother emerges from her den, she will evacuate the anal plug and also a few small, hard fecal lumps. The only evidence of her winter ordeal will be small traces of urine left on the den floor.

During the long winter Little Cub's den is slowly expanded. On the warmer winter days the walls of the den will melt as the body heat of the three warms the inside temperature to above freezing. Now that the cubs are demanding large quantities of milk, the mother occasionally consumes snow and ice from the walls of the den to replenish her depleted supply of body fluids.

High above the snow in their helicopter, an international team of three bear biologists, plus Kingmik, a husky bear dog, anxiously await a chance to land. They have spent the past two weeks waiting for a favorable break in the weather. The biologists spot their goal on a northern Canadian island, and the helicopter makes its descent. Once they have landed, their well-rehearsed plans pay off, and almost immediately Kingmik begins his search for a polar bear den.

Kingmik does his job well, and the biologists quickly find a steaming polar bear air vent. The two men begin to cover the exit with a pile of snow, while the young woman biologist chains the dog, a bear antagonist, to a nearby stake. Once the exit is blocked, the probable location of the maternity chamber is determined and the two men slowly scrape a hole into the den. The female bear, now awake, growls and roars indignantly, hoping to scare the intruders away from her cub and den.

When they finally break into the den, they find the she-bear huddled over her cub in the corner. The three estimate her weight and draw the required amount of immobilizing drug into the syringe they have with them. The she-bear, normally aggressive in such circumstances, will not leave her den because of her cub. Using the powder syringe gun, the bear management and control expert from the Soviet Union shoots the hovering mother in the muscles of the neck.

During the ten-minute latent period, before the drug takes effect, the excited biologists prepare themselves for the work ahead. From their past experiences they know they have a minimum of four safe working hours before the drug begins to wear off. The Canadian naturalist, seeing that the female has ceased moving, decides that the drug must be taking effect. He opens the hole a bit farther and eases into the den. It is less than an hour since the three stepped from the helicopter.

The naturalist helps the young woman into the den. She immediately moves to help the cub, trapped under his mother's shoulder. While the naturalist begins his work, the young woman, a vertebrate zoologist from North Carolina, plays surrogate mother, warming the little fellow inside her heavy parka.

The first order of business for the naturalist is the tagging. Both of the she-bear's ears are pierced, and colored plastic tags are inserted. These numbered tags will someday tell the distance and direction the she-bear has traveled. Using red nitro-enamel dye, the naturalist marks a large number 38 on the animal's back. The numerals will be easily visible from half a mile away.

The management and control expert moves in and extracts a molar that will be sawed in half. By counting the molar's rings, they will be able to tell the age of the female— just as lumberjacks count annual rings in trees to determine their age.

Both men pull the huge bear from her corner and begin recording her measurements. It is next to impossible to weigh these creatures in the wild, so they take body length and the circumference of her belly and apply it to a previously worked-out weight-versus-measurement chart. They find that she weighs approximately 675 pounds. Both blood and milk samples are taken to check protein differences, which would indicate the possibility of various races within their species around the world. Heartbeat, breathing rate, and rectal temperature are taken before their attention is turned to the cub.

Now that the cub has settled down, they quickly measure his temperature, heartbeat, and respiration rate and weigh him. Afraid of deforming his ear, they decide not to tag it.

The two hours they have been in the den have gone quickly. The she-bear is beginning to move her head—a sign that the three must leave soon. As they leave, they try to repair the damage to the den. Even if they do finish the job, the she-bear will probably leave it to find another, safer home, away from these curious intruders.

Back in their helicopter, the three are pleased with their work and hope that someday they will meet number 38 again—alive and healthy.

Little Cub's father is still out on the ice pack, hunting. The polar night has been difficult. The huge he-bear has gone ten days without eating. His fat supply is getting dangerously low in this rigorous weather, and he continues to wander and hunt for food.

For Little Cub's father, living on the ice pack during the winter presents two basic problems—food and warmth. Polar bears, homoiothermic or warm-blooded animals, depend on their well-positioned blubber to insulate them from much of the cold. Blubber, as much as four inches deep, has been found covering a polar bear's rump, an area often in contact with ice and snow. An even layer of fat protects the polar bear's legs while he paddles in the Arctic waters. The hind legs have measurable amounts of fat only on the outside surface; since the hind legs are held together, there is no need for insulation of the inside surface.

Covering the thick blubber is the polar bear's magnificent pelt, long considered an article of beauty by man. The long guard hairs trap a layer of air for further insulation against the cold. The dense inner layer of hair is so thick that water cannot penetrate to the skin. Once the bear has entered the water, the air is displaced, but the skin stays dry. When the bear climbs out of the sea, a quick shake rids the oily, waterproofed hair of the water.

The natural color of a fully grown polar bear is a creamy, yellowish white. Depending on his surroundings and the type of light, he may seem to be more one shade than the other. If it is a brilliant day, he will seem to be more white than yellow. If it is a dark, dreary day, he will appear more yellow than white. Scottish whalers, seeing the yellow-colored polar bear, nicknamed him "Brounie."

When a polar bear falls asleep in the open, his coat easily blends in with the surroundings, the white serving as protective coloration. When the bear is hunting, seals have a difficult time seeing him approach, since the white of his coat blends with the snow. The Eskimos adopt this polar bear camouflage by using a white cloth screen to hide themselves as they sneak up on seals basking in the sun.

The polar bear has held the position as the largest terrestrial carnivore for thousands of years. A mature male measures eight to nine feet long from nose to tail. His weight ranges from 800 to 1000 pounds; there have been accurate reports of polar bears weighing 1450 pounds, and an unreliable report of a male weighing 1600 pounds. A mature female will be smaller than the male, measuring approximately six feet long and usually weighing 700 pounds.

In addition to the polar bear's massive size, he has a well-developed neck and powerful shoulders—necessities in hunting. Many seasoned observers of polar bears contend that when any act of strength is performed, such as killing a seal, the left paw is the one used. Using his teeth and left paw, the bear pulls the seal from his breathing hole, often squeezing the intestines out.

Little Cub awakes. Hungry after sleeping, he tries to suckle but is unable to reach his mother's breast. Her big paw is in his way. Frustrated, he whimpers and cries, but his mother does not hear him. Using his newly developed voice, he tries to growl and roar but ends up screeching. Finally his mother wakes, and he can now suckle himself to sleep.

FEBRUARY
PEKSOK—The Days of Drifting Snow

Little Cub is now two months old. In this short time he has gone from one pound to his present thirteen pounds. His length has more than doubled to over two feet. Like any other infant, Little Cub has begun the painful process of teething. His teeth have already started to break through the tender gums. Very soon incisors will erupt, and he will have the needed teeth to begin the spring hunting season.

Now that February has begun, the days are becoming longer and occasionally the biting cold eases. Little Cub, excited as a boy on his first camping trip, moves to the opposite side of the den and sleeps apart from his mother for the first time. As soon as the cold returns, he hurries back to his mother's warmth.

With both Little Cub and his sister able to walk, even though clumsily, the den becomes busy. As they explore the den, their first encounters with each other are merely mutual sniffing sessions. Once they have sufficiently inspected each other and the den, they begin to play. At first they engage in gentle shoving; then they end up wrestling across the floor.

Little Cub, somewhat stronger than his sister, has the advantage.

After having her ears nipped, Little Cub's sister decides it is time to find her mother. She springs across the den and runs into the big she-bear's back. Awaking with a start, finding her cubs rolling on the floor, their mother firmly pulls them apart and draws them to her breast. Both cubs begin to suckle and then become drowsy. With the den quiet once again, the mother eases back into sleep.

As both the cubs grow larger, their mother is the one that suffers. The she-bear is restricted to living off her fat reserves and the ice and snow from the walls of her den. During her vigil inside the den she loses a large quantity of weight. After three months she begins to look emaciated.

Tracing the ancestry of the polar bear requires an intimate knowledge of every aspect of its present life and, possibly even more important, a wizard-like ability to guess the creature's past history. Very few fossil remains of the polar bear have been found.

With evidence to show that one member of the brown bear family, a close relative of the polar bear, did not set foot on North America until after the most recent glaciation, we may conclude that the polar bear did not originate here. More than likely, the polar bear originated somewhere in Siberia. It is believed that the Asiatic brown bear population split, and this new species was developed.

No matter where the polar bear came from, it is accepted that during the age of the glaciers, perhaps during the mid-Pleistocene, a sizable group of brown bears was isolated from the main population. During this isolation, strong selection pressures forced them to change their style of life.

As it is obvious today, their eating habits changed from a vegetarian diet to one mainly of meat. These evolutionary changes that began thousands of years ago are still going on today. All one has to do is observe the animals' teeth to see the changes in progress. The polar bear has canines from two to three inches long, and premolars specially adapted for killing and eating animal flesh. A polar bear has been credited with biting a half-inch iron spear in two—not the type of teeth a vegetarian would have. The molars in the back of the mouth have degenerated, indicating a general lack of use, due to the polar bear's adaptation to a carnivorous diet. In contrast to those of the brown or black bears, whose diets consist of roots, berries, fruits, insects, and occasionally small game, the rear molars are well developed and flat, adapted to the omnivorous diet.

One of the most revealing facets of the relation between the brown bear and the polar bear has occurred in some of the zoos around the world. When given the opportunity to mate, these two different bears will produce fertile hybrids. This conclusively proves their close relationship in the not-too-far-distant past.

> Of the black bear you need not be afraid,
> But killing white ones is a dangerous trade.
> In this be cool, and well direct your lead,
> And take your aim at either heart or head;
> For struck elsewhere, your piece not level'd true
> Not long you'll live your erring hand to rue.
> —Author unknown

In the sports section of his newspaper, an avid hunter reads the small advertisement: "Come to Alaska and hunt the polar bear." The ad goes on to state that for only two thousand dollars, a polar bear is guaranteed—"while they last." The hunter dreams he is dressed in white, stalking the great bear between the piles of ice and snow. After hours of the chase the bear turns and charges. The hunter, at the last second, stops the bear inches from his feet. Jolted from the dream by his excitement, he immediately sits down and writes the outfitters.

One month later, after a long flight to Alaska, the hunter is flying in a small plane equipped with skis. He and his guide-pilot are searching for polar bear tracks on the snow-covered ice. Not far away a second plane helps them in their search. After half an hour the guide spots tracks, and they follow them until they spot the huge white bear.

The hunter and guide land their plane on the ice. Both men scramble out of the plane and hide behind a ridge. The second plane begins to drive the bear toward the hunter. He quickly prepares his high-powered rifle. When the bear is fifty yards away, the guide instructs the hunter to shoot. He lines up the cross-hairs on the bear and, with one shot, the bear rolls over, dead.

The hunter returns to the plane and climbs back into the warm cockpit. The guide walks to the carcass, checks to see if the bear is dead, and quickly skins it. Once the pelt is off the animal and on the ground, he takes his saw and cuts off the head—promised to a researcher at a school in Anchorage. The guide picks up the pelt and head, leaving the rest of the carcass lying on the ice.

For the guide, it has been a profitable winter. His record book would show that this polar bear is the 146th bear killed so far this winter.

Back home, the hunter tells his friends of his epic adventure and the ferocious polar bear.

Far up the coast of Norway, a sealing vessel pulls out of the Tromsö harbor. In his cabin a polar bear hunter impatiently waits during the voyage north to Svalbard and bear hunting grounds. Even before the ship reaches Svalbard, polar bears are sighted on ice floes.

The hunter is called from his cabin, and the ship slowly moves closer to a bear-laden ice floe. A great he-bear watches this strange, foul-smelling "iceberg" move closer and closer, unaware of his doomed fate. The hunter lies on the deck, aims

Photographs by
Bruce Coleman, Inc.

at the bear, now thirty yards away, and fires. His bear now shot, he returns to his cabin for a victory celebration. The ship moves up to the ice floe, and the bear is hauled on board with the ship's boom.

A beautiful young Scandinavian photographer, capturing the sequence of events, watches sadly as the crew skins the animal. She cannot believe that they discard everything except the hide. Why do they have to kill these beautiful animals, she wonders, when they are such a pleasure to watch.

An amphibious plane circles North and South Twin Island on James Bay. Finding a patch of smooth water, the pilot lands and taxis to South Twin. Having heard that polar bears are often trapped on these islands during the summer, a hunter from the United States begins his hunt. The first day he finds three bears: a male, a female, and her cub. Without much trouble he kills the mother and cub. The next day he kills the male and wounds a fourth bear. For the rest of the summer, no more bears are to be seen on South Twin. In a few days the hunter proceeds to North Twin and kills three more bears. Not wanting to be burdened with the hides, he gives them to his guide.

Each of the three hunting stories is true—a rather sad commentary on our modern relationship with the polar bear. It is hard to understand what these men are thinking as they stalk and eventually kill these beautiful creatures, as they do not need to rely on them as a source of meat or fur. Polar bears and, for that matter, other animals have had illusionary images constructed about them, due to man's desire to create a worthy hunting foe. But the polar bear is generally not a ferocious beast around man, merely curious. The hunter's idea of him is false.

George Sutton, a naturalist living in the Canadian Arctic, describes the feelings associated with hunting the polar bear:

Polar bear hunting . . . isn't always as exciting as you may imagine it to be. You see your bear and walk toward it, wondering all the time why it doesn't run away. Is the brute drunk, or asleep on its feet, or what is the matter? you ask yourself, and then a rifle is raised, you hear a sharp crack! and the bear comes rolling down the rocks. Carrying back great chunks of meat and bundles of hide is gratifying within certain limits, but it becomes drudgery after a while. There ought to be more growling, you think, more running and chasing, a little more excitement. I continued to like bear steak very much, especially the fatty part, but bear hunting frankly palled on me a little.

Before one can condemn or condone the harvesting of polar bears, economic ramifications must be considered. In Alaska and, for that matter, throughout much of the Arctic, the polar bear contributes much to the economy of the region. Hunters are willing to pay large fees for guides and also for the use of their airplanes. The Department of the Interior estimated that in the mid-1960's each polar bear killed contributed a minimum of fifteen hundred dollars to the economy in the form of food, lodging, licenses, guide fees, and equipment. For the three hundred bears known to have been taken during this one-year period, nearly half a million dollars was distributed to small Alaskan villages.

The polar bear's pelt, with its long guard hair and thick underfur, will sell for between three and eight hundred dollars, depending on the condition and size. These pelts are often displayed as rugs or wall hangings. Due to their water resistance and buoyancy, shreds of the pelts are used in the production of fishing flies and lures for commercial sale. If the fur is not in the best condition, the pelt is tanned into high-quality leather.

When transportation is not a problem, the meat of the polar bear is relished. Blubber is eaten and used in a variety of different ways. The gall is utilized in some Arctic areas for medicinal purposes.

Writing in 1967, Vagn Flyger noted the conditions prevailing at that time:

> The annual worldwide harvest of polar bears is approximately 1200 according to reported kills—unreported kills probably do not exceed 300 animals. Biologists have estimated the number of polar bears in existence to be in the range of 15,000–20,000. The annual harvest of about 1500 animals, therefore, is somewhere between 5 per cent and 10 per cent of the population. According to the experts, such a harvest is not excessive; but the experts can be wrong! Some people may remember that one of the world's foremost whale biologists maintained for many years that there was no indication of a decline in whale stocks. This man's opinion weighed heavily in negotiations concerning whales; so heavily that today some of our whale species are almost extinct. The public surely would not wish to risk the possibility of the polar bear's extermination.
>
> In Canada and Greenland only natives are permitted to hunt polar bears. Hunting for sport is entirely forbidden, and non-natives may shoot only in personal defense. At some DEW Line sites there are signs warning the operating personnel: "If you shoot a polar bear in self-defense, remember, he has a better lawyer than you have." All polar bear hunting is forbidden in the U.S.S.R.

As a result of the extensive hunting pressure, the International Union for the Conservation of Nature and Natural Resources has added the polar bear to its list of animals in danger of extinction.

The United States, far from being a leader in the protection of the polar bear or other mammals, has finally moved to the bear's assistance. Recorded in the *Federal Register* is one of conservationists' most rewarding victories—the Marine Mammal Protection Act of 1972. Placed into effect on December 21, 1972, the law restricts the taking, possession, transportation, selling, offering for sale, and importing of marine mammals. Specified as the mammals to be given protection are: the northern sea otter, southern sea otter, Atlantic walrus, Pacific walrus, dugong, west African manatee, west Indian manatee, Amazonian manatee, and the polar bear. In addition to the mammals named, marine mammal products have also been prohibited.

In an effort to preserve their cultural traditions, Indians, Aleuts, and Eskimos residing on the coast of the North Pacific Ocean or the Arctic Ocean may continue to take any marine mammal without a permit. The only restrictions for them are that they take marine mammals for subsistence only, for purposes of creating and selling authentic native articles of handicraft and clothing; that the hunting must not be accomplished in a wasteful manner, and that aircraft cannot be used.

Hunters are not the only ones affected by this edict. Scientists are also under restrictions. A detailed description of any scientific research project in which a marine mammal or its product is to be used must be submitted and approved. If the marine mammal is listed as an endangered species, a detailed justification of the need for such marine mammal, including a discussion of possible alternatives, must be submitted to the Secretary of the Department of the Interior.

Our only hope is that we have not acted too late.

While many people would fight against any compromise in conservation, a proposal issued by Vagn Flyger has been advanced by hunters, and even scientists would probably admit to its value. It states:

> . . . the most exhilarating way to hunt is with a
> gun that fires a syringe filled with an immobilizing

drug. With this weapon the animal is not killed, but is merely drugged into unconsciousness for a short period. In contrast to hunting, where the excitement ends with the squeeze of the trigger, most of the fun begins after the syringe-gun trigger is pulled.

I have experienced many types of hunting, but nothing matches that of catching a live animal. I recommend this as one of the most rewarding sports anywhere in the world. Now modern science and technology have given us new tools and instruments to add to the sportsman's enjoyment, and the time is ripe to switch from lead bullets to projectile syringes.

Catch-them-alive hunters could bring back photographs as evidence of their prowess and, at the same time, contribute to science by marking the polar bears with ear tags before releasing them. Naturally, some of the animals would be killed, because the method is not yet foolproof, but the annual toll would be greatly reduced.

To insure minimum mortality, it would be necessary to give considerable training to the guides. Although many hunters have greatly exaggerated opinions of their own ability, very few know much about their quarry or the out-of-doors; they get their bear because of the knowledge and efficiency of their guide. For this reason, the use of syringe guns would necessitate the training of the guides only.

In this way hunters and scientists could work together, each satisfying his own needs while helping in the conservation of the polar bear.

A strange, mechanical creature crawls across the tundra. Stopping in a likely spot, the seismological team begins to drill a hole into the ice and snow. Once they have finished, they drop their charges underground. With their sensitive equipment turned on, the underground charges are detonated. By studying the micro-earthquake waves, the team can locate substrata bearing oil. With many feet of tape to be deciphered by geologists, the mobile unit turns and retraces its tracks.

Nearby a female polar bear, startled, awakes from her sleep. Hearing the crackling of the diesel engine and the crunching snow, she forgets the two small cubs lying on her breast. In panic she begins frantically to dig out of her den, leaving the two small cubs exposed to the outside air and the icy floor. They die, freezing quickly.

MARCH
NETCHIALOOT—
The Birth Days
of Netchek Seals

March begins with winter's first warm weather. Across Shugliak Island the snowdrifts become soggy. Puddles form across the lakes. At noon the brilliance is blinding. Warmed by the afternoon sun, water flows, later to be frozen in the cold night. Ptarmigan warm themselves in the glare, eyes shut.

Eskimos describe this time of year as the season of the wild wind—so wild that it covers their komatik trails and rips apart the snowdrifts. But most important, it is the peak of the pupping season for the netchek seal.

Little Cub is maturing quickly. He now weighs twenty-eight pounds and is thirty inches long. His sister weighs twenty-five pounds and is twenty-eight inches long. Both cubs, after three months, finally have completely blackened noses, lips, and footpads—just like their mother's. Their tongues and the inside of their mouths now are a bleached violet color.

The past few weeks have been difficult for Little Cub's mother. When they aren't sleeping, both cubs spend every spare moment playing in the den, creating an atmosphere hardly conducive to sleep. The great she-bear has far less fat reserve than she started with in December. Waiting for the right day to break out of the den has been slow and torturous. Before she does, it is essential that the cubs be strong enough to survive in the rigorous Arctic environment. Without enough strength, fatigue will easily set in.

Now that the sunlight lasts longer and longer each day and the weather feels warmer again, she has confidence that the cubs are ready for their first excursion outside their protected home.

Their mother begins the tedious job of digging through the exit she packed more than three months ago. Her months of inactivity make it seem an arduous task. Slowly she breaks through to a blindingly bright day. Both cubs, afraid of this strange, new light, hide in the corner. The big she-bear first beckons to them, but eventually she must return to the inner chamber and nudge the cubs outside with her big snout. After thirteen weeks of darkness their eyes smart.

The first day outside the den, the cubs are so over-whelmed by their strange new world that they do not move from their mother's side. She does not walk far. After tasting some freshly fallen snow, she finds a likely spot and begins to dig for frozen grasses and berries. The grass she does find and eats dulls her long winter hunger.

Once the she-bear has finished eating, the three explore for a short distance. The mother is careful to keep the cubs from becoming too tired. They return to the den before long, and the cubs suckle themselves to sleep.

As the cubs get used to the strangeness of the outside world, they take more and more pleasure in their daily romps outside the den. While their mother is digging for grasses and berries, the two cubs play together, rolling in the snow and fighting mock battles. They climb small hills and slip and roll down again. After a great deal of experimentation they eventually find that sliding down is the most fun.

As they play and slide in the snow, it does not take long before the cubs are hungry. They quickly run to their mother, trying to nurse while standing up. Annoyed, Little Cub's mother finds a suitable spot and lies down to let them nurse. Not interested in sleeping, they soon return to play.

Each day as the cubs become stronger and more confident, the three wander a little farther from the den. Both cubs can now run so fast that it would be difficult for a fleet-footed man to overtake them.

The she-bear's stomach is beginning to awaken after the winter of inactivity. The plants are helping to prepare her system for the seal blubber she will eat once they are on the ice.

During many March days the wind is too cold and the snow too harsh for the mother to take the cubs outside. The three stay inside the den waiting for the next day and more promising weather. On such days the she-bear's patience is heavily tried with her cubs' nonstop play and combat.

Late February and early March are the birth days of the netchek seals. Little Cub's father can now begin his search for the seals' birth chambers. Even though the chambers are on the ice, they are difficult to locate because they look like ordinary snowdrifts. The polar bear must use his sensitive nose to find these musky-smelling chambers.

If one questioned which polar bear sense, sight or smell, is more important, a short period of observation would reveal the answer. The polar bear's eyes appear lazy and tired. Much of the time he seems hardly able to keep them open. His nose is a different matter. To most observers, it is just a dark knob at the end of his snout, but closer scrutiny will show that the two nostrils are never still. Their sharp outlines are continually contorting to catch any hint of a nearby meal.

When he is searching for food, the polar bear travels into the wind at an angle that gives him the widest scenting coverage of the territory. If the wind changes direction, as it often does, he will zigzag back and forth until he has reoriented himself. Polar bears have been attracted by cooking blubber from as far as five to seven miles away. Some people will even credit him with detecting the smell at a distance of ten miles. Many ingenious hunters in search of polar bears have saved themselves treacherous journeys by luring the bears to their ship or camp with burning blubber.

Factors that cannot be overlooked when discussing the relative value of two different senses are the environmental conditions present in the Arctic. During sunny days the glare from the ice and snow would blind almost any pair of eyes. Windblown snow can also seriously impair vision. But these conditions do not limit the polar bear's scenting powers in this inorganic, desolate wasteland.

Once a seal's birth chamber has been found, the he-bear, using his forepaw, quickly scrapes off as much of the hard-packed dome as possible. Now that the icy den has been exposed, the huge bear rears on his hind legs and pounces with his forepaws as hard as possible. The inner portion of the drift is a bell-shaped ice chamber, surprisingly thick. Not successful the first time, he walks away, then turns around and charges. Ten feet from the target, he springs and pounces again. With every ounce of his thousand pounds directed at the chamber, he finally breaks through. Inside and alone, the cream-colored netchek seal pup lies waiting for his mother. Disappointed with only the pup—hardly a decent meal—the polar bear sweeps him into the seal's breathing hole. The mother seal, immediately noticing her pup bobbing in the breathing hole, streaks to his rescue. Just as the seal surfaces to help her pup, the great he-bear swiftly draws the mother out of the hole with his left paw. In one great motion, the seal is out of the water, on the ice, and dead. Little Cub's father eats his long-sought meal.

The polar bear's paw serves him well. The soles of his feet are densely covered with short hairs. When he nears a seal's breathing hole, his furred paws muffle his approach. Once a seal has made his appearance, the paw acts as a grappling hook to help pull the seal out of his hole. A male polar bear, weighing a thousand pounds, will have a hind paw measuring eighteen inches long and thirteen inches wide. Robert Peary once observed: "About a mile from the shore, a broad track, like the trail of a man on snowshoes, was seen winding down the slope ahead of us: the huge plantigrade footprints of a polar bear."

Records of polar bear paws, cut off at the ankle, weighing fifty pounds, have been reported. With his tremendous strength and huge paws, it is no wonder that bear-proof storage vaults are difficult to construct. Climbing up pressure ridges, the bear can cling with his black claws to the finest fractures across the ice; the paws prevent him from sliding.

Once his meal is finished, the great he-bear moves away from the scene of his dinner. As he leaves, he begins a routine dating back to his days as a cub. His ponderous walk turns into skips and ends in great leaps off the ice. The great leaps are followed by a circular chase that makes him dizzy. He somersaults to the ground and lies on his back, sparring with the sky. Then, up on his feet again, he chases himself around a ridge of ice. Unable to catch his imaginary playfellow, he finds a protected spot and falls asleep.

For many years the polar bear has been accused of being a stupid animal. Most of the accusations have stemmed from his lack of fear in the presence of men. Vilhjalmur Stefansson, writing in the early 1900's, stated:

. . . their unwary approach to a party of men and dogs must not be set down against them as lack of intelligence. They simply have not the data upon which to reason, for they have never before encountered any dangerous animals upon the ice.

The polar bear is not an animal easy to trick. Fridtjof Nansen described a polar bear's reluctance to steal the bait from a trap:

> He looked well at the apparatus, then raised himself cautiously on his hind legs and laid his right paw on the cross-beam just beside the trap, stared for a little, hesitating, at the delicious morsel, but did not at all like the ugly jaws round it. But the bear shook his head suspiciously, lowered himself cautiously onto all-fours again and snuffed carefully at the wire that the trap was fastened by, following it all along to where it was made fast to a great block of ice. He went round this, and saw how cleverly it was all arranged, then slowly followed the wire back, raised himself as before, with his paw on the beams of the gallows, had a long look at the trap, and shook his head again.

Back on Shugliak Island, an old he-bear, Little Cub's grandfather, awakes from his winter sleep. He sluggishly digs himself out of his snow shelter. The winter has been particularly long and severe for the bear. The old, emaciated bear, now impotent, immediately digs for some grasses and berries. Once he has eaten and feels stronger, the trek to the ice begins. Not far away another polar bear begins his journey to the ice. Unfortunately, both hungry he-bears meet. An immediate display of growls and intimidating charges ends quickly and is replaced by a brutal battle. Even with years of fighting experience, Little Cub's grandfather is no match for the bloodthirsty, starved attacker. An unseen blow knocks the old bear down. The attacker wastes no time in ending the struggle. The cannibal finishes his sordid meal and continues his journey. How true the old saying that biologists often repeat—no wild animal dies of old age. Old age is a luxury left to human beings and a few of their domesticated animals.

Traditionally, the Eskimo has hunted the polar bear with a lance. It was not until recently that guns were introduced to the Eskimo's culture.

When a polar bear's trail is found, the Eskimos stop and carefully observe his tracks. Having had much experience with hunting the great bear, the Eskimos know that it must be a male, because of its large tracks. The direction and the speed are easily calculated. Most important, the tracks are very fresh.

It has been less than an hour since the bear passed by. The Eskimos drive their team of huskies as hard as they can; the huskies pull the sled over the ice at a speed of close to twenty miles an hour. As they pass around a pressure ridge, the bear is quickly spotted. The Eskimos slash the walrus-hide trace lines, and the huskies streak after the bear. Now realizing that he has been pursued, the great he-bear turns and runs from the dogs.

The normal manner in which the polar bear moves can be characterized as a weighty shuffle. One would not suspect that a thousand-pound he-bear is able to move very rapidly, but he can cover ground much faster than expected. When he is chased by a team of huskies, he will gallop at a speed reaching twenty-five miles an hour.

Having surprised the bear, the huskies quickly catch up to him. Nipping ferociously at the bear's hindquarters, the huskies bring the polar bear to bay. One of the dogs, a little overzealous, tries to confront the huge beast. The bear hits him up in the air with his huge paw. The husky lands on the ground fifteen feet away, his neck broken.

Although the dogs can bring the bear to bay, they cannot kill him themselves. With the huskies circling the bear, intimidating him, the Eskimos have time to run up to the field of battle. Once again the Eskimo confronts Nanook—the great white polar bear.

The two hunters spread apart. The first Eskimo, feinting, pretends to thrust his lance at the bear's left side. When the bear turns to defend himself from the deceptive move, the second Eskimo wheels with all his might and thrusts his lance into the unprotected right side. Mortally wounded, the bear tries to resist his attackers, but falls and dies.

One of the Eskimos gathers the dogs and begins the long walk back to the komatik, or sled. The other begins to skin the bear. By the time the other Eskimo has returned, the bear has been skinned and great chunks of meat and blubber are being sliced off. After the bear has been butchered, all that is left are the bones, liver, and some of the entrails. The two Eskimos return to their villages and provide their community with bear meat and blubber.

Eskimos have long had a reputation for telling exaggerated tales of epic proportion and believing in many unfounded taboos. Eskimos believe that many taboos must be observed if one is to be successful in hunting the polar bear. The Eskimos of Southampton Island would beg forgiveness before they kill polar bears and forbid the women of their camp to comb their hair on the day of a bear hunt. The Frobisher Bay Eskimos would hang the dead polar bear's inflated bladder on their tent or boat for three days—the bladder of a male bear decorated with men's instruments and the female bear with women's jewelry. They also believe the skull of any animal should not be crushed while hunting in order to insure continued success.

Vilhjalmur Stefansson summarizes the reasons Eskimos give for polar bears allowing themselves to be killed by men:

> . . . polar bears are unable to make for themselves
> certain tools which they need. What the male bears

especially value are crooked knives and bow-drills, and the female bears are especially eager to get women's knives, skin scrapers, and needle-cases; consequently when a polar bear has been killed, his soul accompanies the skin into the man's house and stays with the skin for several days (among most tribes, for four days if it is a male bear, for five days if it is a female). The skin during this time is hung up at the rear end of the house, and with the skin are hung up the tools which the bear desires, according to the sex of the animal killed. At the end of the fourth or fifth day the soul of the bear is by a magic formula driven out of the house, and when it goes away it takes with it the souls of the tools which have been suspended with it and uses them thereafter.

There are certain manners and customs of humanity which are displeasing to polar bears, and for that reason those customs are carefully abjured during the period when the soul of the bear is in the man's house. The bear, in other words, is treated as an honored guest who must not be offended. If the bear's soul has been properly treated during his stay with the man, and if he has received the souls of implements of good quality, then he will report those things in the land of the polar bears to which he returns, and other bears will be anxious to be killed by so reliable a man. If the wives of certain hunters are careless about treating the souls of the bears properly while they are in their houses, this will offend the bears quite as much as if the man who killed them had done it, and this may cause an excellent hunter to get no polar bears at all. Certain women are known in their communities for this very undesirable quality, and if a woman becomes a widow, her reputation for carelessness in treating the souls of animals may prevent her from getting a good second husband.

Even with their many taboos, Eskimos are skilled and crafty hunters. Canadian "Mountie" Montague described a polar bear rocking on an ice floe:

I watched Ee-kalak (an Eskimo) sit for hours one day studying a bear "acting up" upon an ice floe some distance from the shore, but not beyond rifle shot. "Why does not one kill Nanook?" I asked.

"One awaits better luck," Ee-kalak answered, and I sat down to watch the native in my turn. Presently a seal broke water; the bear darted after him, cuffed him dead, and then swam back to the ice-pan to push the seal up on it. With the free paw the bear crushed the seal's head. The native smiled at me as the echo of his rifle shot died away, and he spoke: "With a little patience one obtains both a Nanook and a *puyee* [seal] with one bullet."

The Eskimos have known for thousands of years that the polar bear's liver is poisonous both to humans and to their dogs. As the Arctic was first being explored, many of the travelers, upon eating the liver, experienced the effects of the poison.

In 1597, Barents and his men were stranded while on an expedition to Novaya Zemlya. Suffering from scurvy and lack of meat, they shot a polar bear and removed the liver:

[We] drest and eate it, the taste liked us well, but it made us all sicke, specially three that were exceeding sicke, we verily thought that we should have lost them, for all their skin come off, from the foote to the head, but yet they recovered againe, for which we give God heartie thanks.

Later, Dr. E. K. Kane wrote in his journal:

October 8, 1854, when I was out in the *Advance* with Captain Dehaven, I satisfied myself that it was a vulgar prejudice to regard the liver of the bear as poisonous. I ate of it freely myself and succeeded in making it a favorite dish with the mess. The cub's liver was my supper last night, and today I have the symptoms of poison in full measure—vertigo, diarrhoea, and their concomitants.

It was not until recently that what had been known for thousands of years in the Eskimo's Arctic was just proved in the laboratory of intelligent men. Chemical analysis of the polar bear's liver showed that the concentration of vitamin A was so high that it would be toxic to humans when ingested.

In addition to liver poisoning, Eskimos, particularly in the Canadian Arctic, have been afflicted with parasites after eating polar bear meat that was not thoroughly cooked. More than 50 per cent of the polar bear meat that has been studied was infected with Trichinella larvae—that microscopic nematode so often associated with uncooked pork.

It has been found that Trichinella is transmitted to the polar bear from seals. Minute, scavenging invertebrates called amphipods are eaten by both the ringed and bearded seals. Amphipods feed on the carcasses of previously infected mammals while floating in the ocean. When the seals feed on the swarming amphipods, they receive the parasites from both the undigested contents of the amphipods' digestive system and also the bits of meat they accidentally consume along with the invertebrates. Once the seal is infected, the circle is completed when the polar bear catches and eats the parasitized seal meat.

Little Cub has been spending the past three weeks in and out of his den. Following his mother as she forages for grasses, he has grown stronger from all of the exercise—walking in the deep snow and playing with his sister. Little Cub's mother has decided that the two cubs are ready to begin the long trek to the ice. Now, the third week in March, they finally abandon their den for the remainder of winter.

Only fifteen inches from the top of his shoulder to the ground, Little Cub has difficulty marching through the snow.

When the snow is not very deep, both cubs follow their mother in single file, using the huge bear paw tracks as a well-broken path. If the snow becomes too deep, the cubs move up alongside the hulky she-bear in order not to fall into the deep tracks—Little Cub learned quickly that once he fell into one of his mother's tracks, the only way to get out was to cry for her help while doing an uncomfortable headstand.

Even though both cubs have demonstrated a surprising ability to climb over the difficult terrain, they have to rest often. Little Cub's mother finds a big rock to break the freezing wind, and the three, lying together, rest. The mother-bear warms and suckles her two cubs to a restful sleep. When the sky is clear, the three bask in the sun, waiting for their aching muscles to regain their strength.

After their naps Little Cub and his sister start to scrap. They chase each other around the rocks and across the snow-drifts. Their mother, now awake, begins to chase after them. At first she teases and spars with them, pretending to fight. She finally leads them to the top of a small snow-covered hill and tumbles down to the bottom. Following their mother's demonstration, the two cubs roll down after her.

Close to the northernmost point of Shugliak Island, another mother and her cubs are beginning their journey to the ocean. Tramping through the snow, they also leave the maternity den they slept in throughout the long winter. A pack of polar wolves suddenly appear. Since they were upwind of the bears, the mother was unable to catch the wolves' scent and evade them. The pack quickly surrounds the three bears. The two cubs hide underneath the mother, not knowing quite what to do. The three wolves, each more than one hundred and fifty pounds, take turns intimidating the she-bear. Normally, wolves would never dare to threaten a grown bear, but now, with her cubs hidden beneath her, the mother is vulnerable. The tense game continues back and forth—growls against snarls. The mother swings her huge paw at one wolf's daring, lunging strike. For a moment a poorly hidden cub is exposed. The second wolf snaps his massive jaw and rips the cub's neck. Seriously injured, the small cub lies helplessly on the snow. Incensed by the smell of blood, the wolves drive the she-bear and the other cub away. The she-bear can do nothing for her injured cub—the survivors walk away from the agonizing scene.

Little Cub, his mother, and his sister continue their trek to the ice. Their mother makes sure neither of the cubs overtires. When they do show signs of being tired, the mother nudges them between their hind legs with her muzzle to push them along. If they are exhausted, she will carry one or the other on her back.

In front of them a single trail of bear tracks crosses their path. The she-bear quickly gathers her cubs close to her. She sniffs the trail for ten feet one way and reverses to go ten feet the other way. The cubs, sensing the danger from their mother, remain still. The she-bear stands on her hind legs, dwarfing the cubs. She scans the immediate area but is unable to see or scent the wandering bear. Taking no chances with her cubs, Little Cub's mother quickly leads them away from the trail.

Now a safe distance away, the very tired bears find a hollow spot beneath a high cliff. The she-bear excavates a smooth bed and lies down in the wind-protected space. The two cubs dig into their mother's breast for the milk-producing nipple. Once again the cubs suckle themselves to a needed sleep.

APRIL
TERRIGLULLIOOT—
The Birth Days
of Oogjook Seals

A small fleck, following the eastern shore of Hudson Bay, rides the warm wind from the south. Making its way northward, dipping and rising over the land, it finally sights the important landmark it has waited for so long. Very gradually the small fleck turns to the northwest and begins the lonesome flight over the hungry mouth of Captain Henry Hudson's Bay.

After long hours of solitary flying, the bird's large white patched wings and short tail begin carving a descent to its long-awaited home. The short, descending whistle announces the arrival of the snow bunting on Shugliak Island. Winter cannot last much longer with the advent of the snow bunting. Warm summer days must now be approaching.

The weather tries its best to discourage spring. Sleety rain falls, stops, and changes to a gale of blowing snow. Now covered by new snow, spring must start over again.

April is the month of mating for the polar bears on Shugliak Island. Beginning in March, the mating season continues as late as August in some cases.

A female polar bear marches down the snow-covered eastern coast of Shugliak Island. Now in heat, she marks her trail often with her musky-smelling yellow urine, leaving a scented trail for her prospective suitors. Mating in alternate years, female polar bears are known to remain fertile until the age of twenty-five years.

Unknown to her, two males, following this path, have already begun their search for the female.

One of these trailing males is Little Cub's father. With the polar bear's family alliance lasting for only a very short time, he is now ready to sire another set of cubs with a new female.

As the two males are drawn toward the female, they encounter each other on the trail. Irritable moods and aggressive behavior explode. As in any species of animals, when two males, seeking the same female, meet, a violent confrontation usually follows.

Trying to assert his dominance, Little Cub's father challenges the other bear with a bone-shaking roar. Growls of promised battle are matched back and forth. Neither Little Cub's father nor his contender will flinch from the other's insults. Both have fully committed themselves to fight.

As the fight begins, they act like two prizefighters in the first round, feeling each other out, trying to find the other's weakness.

Little Cub's father takes the initiative and begins the serious fighting. He charges at his opponent and tries to bite his neck. The two fence back and forth, mouths wide open. Little Cub's father suddenly pushes forward and then pounds his massive paw on his opponent's head. Momentarily stunned, the pounded bear cannot prevent his attacker from sinking his long canines into his shoulder. He tries to pull away, but he is unable to free himself from the strong grip of his attacker's jaw. Finally he rolls over, and Little Cub's father must release his teeth. Now that they are both rolling on the ground, they look like kittens playing on the floor. But growls, claws, and teeth tell the real story of what is going on as they tumble together.

For almost two hours their combat continues. Little Cub's father, during most of the fight, seems to be in control. Except for explosive bursts set off by painful prods, his opponent can claim little success. Finally Little Cub's father systematically humiliates his opponent with his teeth and claws. Having had enough, the opponent tries to run. As he runs, the victor, making sure the loser never forgets this bout, digs his claws into the vanquished bear, raking his hindquarters over and over. Satisfied with his efforts, Little Cub's father calmly licks his own wounds.

Afraid of further reprisals, the loser does not stop until he is certain that he is far enough away. Totally exhausted, he cannot stop panting. Finally he is able to assess the damage. Most of one canine tooth has broken off. The holes in his shoulders are oozing blood onto his thick coat, dotting the white with splotches of red. His hindquarters are slashed and painfully red. Worst of all, his paw has been punctured, and it will keep him limping for days.

Little Cub's father resumes his quest of the female. By the next day he is able to overtake her.

The exact details of the mating ceremony have never been witnessed by man. There are a number of theories suggesting that the two find a suitable cave and spend three or four days together. Other theories infer that they mate very quickly and then continue on their way.

From postmortem examinations on a number of male polar bears, it has been found that the penis bone has been at one time fractured and subsequently mended at odd angles. This fracture would tend to indicate that the polar bear's sex act might be a vigorous affair.

An interesting footnote can be added to shed some light on the relationship between the male and female polar bear during mating season. If the two have paired and the female is killed, the male will stay near her side. He-bears have been seen nuzzling their dead mate, unwilling to leave her side. There is one case of a male remaining next to his dead mate throughout a four-day blizzard, not leaving her even to hunt for food. When the hunter attempted to retrieve the carcass, the male defended her body, attacking the man until the male bear was eventually killed.

Little Cub, his mother, and his sister awake from their sleep and continue their trek to the ice. While their mother forages for grasses and berries, the two cubs find another icy slope and climb to the top. In their first attempt they try to slide sedately down the slope but end up tumbling like two snowballs. Their next try is successful—with legs spread out, they slide down the hill on their bellies. By the time they have reached the bottom, both have snowplowed a heap of snow in front of them, concealing their faces with a cover of snow. Over and over, while their mother eats, the two constantly scrap, wrestle, tumble, slide, play, and have fun.

Now that their mother has finished her morning meal, they continue toward the sea. Between each stop they travel any distance from a few hundred yards to half a mile. With the onset of cold weather they will stop more often. Their mother will excavate a circular bed in the snow one or two feet deep. Here she will nurse the cubs and keep them warm. With the cold temperatures, the cubs will spend much of their time curled up in her fur or standing on top of the female, off the cold snow.

At the age of four months Little Cub weighs close to fifty-five pounds. With his frequent feedings, he is thriving. Polar bears living in the wild have been noted for the successful upbringing of their cubs. This is due both to the mothers' indulgent care and to the cubs' tenacious hold on life.

After a few more days of traveling the three bears finally reach the outer edge of the ice sheet that surrounds the entire island. Once again the cubs are awed by their new, strangely beautiful world. At the edge of the ice a dark blue cloud of vapor gathers over the open water. Ice floes float into the island and grind against the stationary ice. In front of them lie miles of floating ice slowly pushed by the northern currents.

The floes and open water increase the hunger of Little Cub's mother for the craved seal blubber. It will not be long before the cubs have their first taste of seal hunting.

Their mother carefully parallels the edge of the land-locked ice, leading the cubs northward. She chooses the path with care; she does not want her cubs to have to swim in the twenty-seven-degree Arctic water just yet. Traveling a sinuous path, the three work their way farther north along the shore. When she finds a protective ridge of ice away from the open water, the mother lies down and suckles the cubs to sleep.

Early the next morning Little Cub's mother leads the two cubs on their first seal hunt. This being *Terriglullioot,* the birth days of the Oogjook seals, there are numerous birth chambers on the ice. Now walking on an ice-locked bay, the three begin searching the leeward edges of the ice ridges. Her head down, the mother tries to sniff out the musky-smelling chambers. The two cubs follow her, trying to mimic her every move, not knowing quite what they are looking for.

After two long hours the mother catches the scent of a birth chamber. Slowly she crawls toward it. With both cubs right behind her, she sits motionless, sizing up the drift. Then she quickly clears the pile of snow from the upper layer and exposes the ice-covered chamber. Standing on her hind legs, she springs and pounces with her forelegs on the chamber. With all her weight pressing on the chamber, the den easily collapses. Hiding inside is a young Oogjook seal. Little Cub's mother scrapes the seal out of the chamber and in the same motion finishes it off. The two cubs are ready for action. Seeing their mother playing, they attack the seal pup, pulling at its flippers. Amused by her cubs' antics, she begins her long-awaited meal. Unwilling to eat the seal's blubber, the cubs crawl beneath their mother to find her milk-producing nipples.

With last night's fresh snow cover and today's unusually calm, bright weather, both men know it will be an excellent day. The helicopter pilot revs his engine and begins to ease off the ground. It took three hours of preheating before the cold engine would start, but now it is ready. The other man sitting next to the pilot, an official from the Alaska Department of Fish and Game, prepares his equipment.

The two are beginning a project of marking polar bears for population studies along the northern coast of Alaska. From Point Barrow they begin to fly east toward the Colville River. At an altitude of three hundred feet, they travel for twenty minutes before spotting any tracks. Turning northward, the tracks lead to broken ice, so they must start their search again. The tracks are becoming more numerous. Finally, after following a trail of fresh tracks, the men sight a polar bear.

The biologist quickly estimates the bear's weight and draws the correct amount of Sernylan, an immobilizing drug, into the syringe. Seeing this strange, noisy bird, the bear begins to run. In many areas polar bears have been subjected to such repeated contact with aircraft that many of the bears completely ignore them. The pilot positions the helicopter and prevents the bear from heading for open water. Running straight inland, the helicopter can easily track the fleeing animal. With the syringe loaded into the powder-charge syringe gun, the biologist opens the door and leans outside the flying helicopter as far as he can. From a range of forty feet, the syringe is shot into the bear's rump.

Immediately the helicopter veers off and circles from a distance of half a mile away. Unless the bear heads for open water or thin ice, they will patiently wait ten minutes for him to become immobilized.

The short history of attempts to immobilize polar bears has been rather sad. Beginning in 1965, of the first nine bears which were drugged, four died and only one was successfully tagged. Since then many immobilizing experiments have been made—many successful, some not. One of the most difficult problems has been finding the right drug. Because of their size and their body chemistry, bears are not easily immobilized. If too little of the immobilizing drug is administered, the bear would not be docile enough to handle. When too much of the drug is used, the bear may die. Much research and experimentation was carried on before a satisfactory drug was found.

The technique of shooting the bear has also taken time to perfect. It was often thought that running the bear was a good way to tire him out and thus ease the process of marking. However, as this was often done during the summer with snowmobiles or fixed winged aircraft, many of the bears became overheated, and this condition, combined with the immobilizing drug, taxed their systems to the point of death. Attempts were made to immobilize the bears in the water, but a number of them, unable to swim any longer once the drug took effect, drowned.

Even when newly perfected techniques and drugs are used, accidents cannot always be prevented. Syringes have been accidentally shot into the bear's chest cavity. With the lung penetrated, death quickly follows. There have been cases of polar bears slowly suffocating while they are drugged, because of mucous blockage in the bronchial tubes.

Stimulated by these unfortunate accidental deaths of polar bears, trophy hunters are quick to react when scientists tamper with animals they assume to be their private property. Hunters resent having fewer bears to pursue. Many hunters fail to realize that these bear biologists are interested in finding ways to preserve rather than to destroy the species. Techniques such as immobilizing bears for marking are essential if we are to gain an understanding of the various facets of the polar bear's life history. The scientists, no doubt, have great remorse over the polar bears' deaths. By reporting these deaths, even though it left them open to heated criticism, they at least made it possible for others to avoid making the same errors, thus saving the lives of many polar bears in the future.

After ten minutes the helicopter moves in. With the bear no longer moving, they do not have to administer any more of the drug. The biologist tags the bear with a monel metal tag on one ear and a nylon tag on the other. Each tag has a number and is marked: "$25 Reward—Return to Fish and Game, Barrow, Alaska, USA." The bear is tattooed on the upper lip and groin with numbers that will further identify him in case the tags are lost. A collar almost two inches wide, made of nylon parachute material, is wrapped around the bear's neck to aid in identification.

Weight is measured by a new method devised by the biologist. Both the pilot and the biologist roll the bear onto a large net and attach the net to the scale on the bottom of the helicopter. Very slowly the helicopter lifts off the ground and the weight is read—952 pounds. The helicopter eases down to the ground again, and the bear is rolled off the net. Using a toothbrush, the men paint the number 19 on his back so he can be identified from a distance. As they leave the site, the men ascertain the exact location of the tagging by a radar location fix from the Distant Early Warning station in Barrow.

Little Cub's father, his mating drive abating, must now try to satisfy his enormous hunger. Having traveled a great distance to find a mate, he is now stranded on Shugliak Island with no food. As he crosses the island on his way to the sea, the scent of seal blubber stops him. Pivoting, he heads toward the tempting smell. Now that it is night, a small flickering light can be seen in the distance. Along with the smell of the seal blubber, he catches the strange odor of man. Staying downwind of the light, he quietly moves into the camp. The seal smell leads him to a small tent. Using his sharp claws, he shreds the side of the tent and crawls inside. The seal blubber, just stripped from the carcass, is ravenously eaten. Unable to control his curiosity, he shatters a keg of salt and paws through the contents. The camp is awakened. Dogs begin to bark, and men grab their guns. Little Cub's father, now frightened, turns to leave the tent. As he leaves, his shoulder knocks over a pile of supplies. Everyone speeds after the bear. Running as best he can with a full stomach, the he-bear leaves the camp, bullets almost keeping him there permanently.

Stefansson describes his experience with marauding polar bears:

> Without doubt the bear is able to tell the difference between a living seal and the meat of a dead one when he sniffs them in the air. There is always seal meat in our baggage and the smell is always about the camp. When a bear passes to leeward he must perceive the many camp odours, but the only one which interests him is that of the seal meat. Knowing no fear, he comes straight into camp, walking leisurely because he does not expect the dead seals which he smells to escape him; neither has he in mind any hostility or disposition to attack, for, through long experience with foxes and gulls, he expects any living thing he meets to make way for him. But if on coming within a hundred or two hundred yards of camp he happens to see a sleeping dog, and especially if the dog were to move slightly, as is common enough, the bear apparently thinks, "Well, that is a live

seal after all!" He then instantly makes himself unbe-
lievably flat on the ice, and with neck and snout touching
the snow advances almost toboggan-fashion toward the
dogs, stopping dead if one of them moves, and advancing
again when they become quiet. If there is any uneven-
ness on the ice, as in the vicinity of our camp, he will
take cover behind a hummock and advance in its
shelter.

If a dog begins barking, the bear immediately loses
interest, apparently thinking it is not a seal, but a fox or
a gull. His mind reverts to the seal meat he has been
smelling. He gets up from his flat position and resumes
his leisurely walk toward the camp.

Having built what they thought was a polar-bear-proof
cache, Dr. E. K. Kane described the ruin of their supplies:

. . . these tigers of the ice seemed to have scarcely
encountered an obstacle. The final cache, which I relied
so much upon, was entirely destroyed. It had been built
with extreme care, of rocks which had been assembled
by very heavy labor, and adjusted with much aid often
from capstanbars as levers. The entire construction was,
so far as our means permitted, most effective and resist-
ing. Not a morsel of pemmican remained except in the
iron cases which, being round with conical ends, defied
both claws and teeth. They had rolled and pawed them
in every direction, tossing them about like footballs, although over eighty pounds in weight. An alcohol case,
strongly iron-bound, was dashed into small fragments
and a tin can of liquor mashed and twisted almost into a
ball. The claws of the beast had perforated the metal, and
torn it up as with a cold chisel.

They had made a regular frolic of it, rolling our
bread barrels over the ice-foot and into the broken outside ice; and, unable to masticate our heavy India-rubber
cloth, they had tied it up in unimaginable hard knots.

As noted by Richard Perry:

> The advent of Europeans in polar seas brought new kinds of food and materials into the lives of polar bears, and opportunities to satisfy their liking for sweetmeats. Tins or boxes are opened with their teeth, despite injury to their gums and jaws, and the contents spread over a wide area, or the tins are tossed aside if the bears cannot open them. The items of food which a hungry bear considers edible are as remarkable as his insatiable curiosity. Fat-stuffs, smoked flesh, dried (but not frozen) fish, cheese, biscuits, bread, raisins, flour, grapes and tobacco, not to mention rope-yard, mackintosh sheeting and adhesive tape, are all sampled. Haig-Thomas followed one cache-rifling bear who, after several miles, excreted intact, though unwound, a spool of photographic film; while wolves, which cleaned up the cache after the bear had finished, had chewed the tins of film until they resembled sponges.

Polar explorers and hunters have often attempted to set up stocks of food or quantities of freshly harvested meat only to have their supplies pilfered by marauding polar animals. For many of the same reasons, the polar bear does not attempt to set up caches of food. Without fail, the Arctic fox, packs of wolves, and even other polar bears would raid food caches. With the great distances traveled by the polar bear, a cache of food would be more of a burden than a benefit.

Little Cub's mother climbs a ridge of ice to inspect the surrounding area. She has done this often since they have been on the ice, making sure she and her cubs are not surprised by a predator. If she does see or smell something to be wary of, she leads the cubs on a sinuous course away from the threat. The only real danger on the ice is an occasional wandering he-bear or, even more infrequently, the bull walrus. As soon as the cubs are old enough to leave, the three will avoid the land to prevent a confrontation with a pack of wolves. The she-bear would much prefer hiding with the cubs in order to escape a dangerous situation, but if she is forced into a fight, a polar bear mother will not back down.

From the descriptions of early Arctic explorers and travelers, it is evident that the polar bear population has declined in the past hundred years. Hunters have taken a high toll, reducing the number of polar bears or even eliminating them completely from some areas. The polar ice cap has receded, making the appearance of polar bears in the southern portions of their range, such as southeastern Greenland and Iceland, quite rare.

The world population of the polar bear has been placed anywhere between five thousand and twenty thousand. Other estimates have placed the number at approximately ten thousand, which includes the six thousand that are supposedly living in Canada.

The task of estimating the polar bear population is formidable. With the polar bear's range extending around the northern polar region, there is much territory to cover. The problem is made more difficult by the bear's white-colored pelt, resulting in low visual contrast between the bear and snow, and the bear's habit of seeking shelter in either a den or under protective cover. Heat-sensitive infrared scanning equipment is now being used in the attempt to locate polar bears in the Arctic regions. Once this infrared system is employed throughout the Arctic, estimates of the polar bear population should be more precise.

Tony Paro, the Fish and Game Commission biologist, returns to his office in Barrow, Alaska. Exhausted after spending the day marking polar bears, he puts his feet up on his desk and reads an article being passed around the office:

The system being developed by NASA to follow bears and other moving objects is called the Interrogation, Recording, and Location System. In its ultimate form it will enable the satellite to interrogate some 32,000 "platforms" (bears, ocean buoys, balloons, and variety of other units), accurately fixing their position at least twice a day and recording other data they transmit.

Let us consider the case of a single polar bear that has been instrumented to communicate with a satellite. At a specified time, when the satellite is expected to be over the bear, the satellite broadcasts a signal that will turn on the bear's transmitter if the animal is within the signal beam. Once the transmitter is on, it returns a signal to the satellite. Because the position of the satellite is known at all times, and the distance between the satellite and the bear can be computed from the length of time it takes the radio signals to travel between them, it is possible to calculate the position of the bear by triangulation after two communications with the animal about three minutes apart. The location data and any other information the bear's communication system has been programmed to provide are stored in the satellite and periodically sent to ground stations, from which they are transmitted to a computer for processing.

Step by step, the sequence proceeds as follows. The set of interrogations that the satellite will conduct on a given orbit is worked out by the computer, and a punched tape is prepared so that the entire set can be transmitted to the satellite when it passes over its command station. A command for a single interrogation has two parts: (1) the address, or radio code, that has been assigned to the platform (in this case a bear), and (2) the exact orbital time at which the interrogation is to be conducted.

At the stipulated time the satellite begins transmitting the address. If the bear is within the range of the signal, the radio unit on the bear receives the signal, decodes it for comparison with the address assigned to the bear and, if the signal corresponds to the address, verifies the platform's identity to the satellite. The satellite then signals the platform to begin transmitting whatever data it is programmed to provide. In the case of a bear the data would presumably be physiological. The entire exchange takes about three seconds.

The results of all the interrogations are stored in the satellite. On completion of an orbit the ground station commands the satellite to transmit the data it has stored. When the satellite has sent all the data, it automatically signals the ground station to that effect. The satellite is then ready to accept a new set of interrogations.

The data received at the ground station are given some further processing there and then transmitted to a central data-processing unit at NASA's Goddard Space Flight Center in Maryland. There the location of each platform is computed and the information obtained from the platform is distributed to the people who want it. The Goddard computer also generates the next set of interrogations for the satellite.

The location function is predicated on the fact that the location of the satellite is precisely known at all times. Hence the distance from the satellite to the point on the ground directly below the satellite is known at any instant. That distance represents one side of a right triangle.

The hypotenuse of the triangle is the line from the satellite to the platform. Its length can be computed from the time required for the special signal generated in the satellite to reach the platform, be generated and return to the satellite—traveling at the speed of light. With the length of two sides of the right triangle known, the length of the third side can be calculated. The third side is the hypothetical line on the ground from the platform to the point directly below the satellite. That line constitutes the radius of a circle. The complete calculation establishes that the bear is somewhere on the circumference of the circle.

In order to establish exactly where the animal is, another exchange of signals between the satellite and the bear is required. It takes place about three minutes after the first exchange. By means of the second exchange another imaginary circle, with the bear on the circumference, is described on the ground. The two circles intersect at two places. The bear is at one of these places. Since one knows where the bear was during the satellite's previous orbit (or where the animal was captured, in the case of the first orbit in which its location was determined), it is not hard to decide which intersection represents the location of the bear; the two intersections are normally hundreds of miles apart. The precision of the technique is sufficient to determine the location of the bear to within about a mile.

It will be well within the capacity of a satellite system to provide information not only about the migration of polar bears, but also on such matters as their respiration and heart action under various circumstances. With such data it would be possible to relate the activity of polar bears to weather conditions on the polar ice cap and thus to come to a better understanding of how an animal can survive in the harsh conditions regularly encountered by the polar bear. Perhaps some of this information will be useful to men who are obliged to adapt themselves to living under Arctic conditions.

The Nimbus satellite, which will be used primarily for oceanography and meteorology, is being designed to orbit the earth from pole to pole at an altitude of about 600 miles. During a single 24-hour rotation of the earth, the satellite will pass over every point on the earth twice —once as it moves from south to north, and again, 12 hours later, as it moves from north to south and the point has rotated to that side of the orbit. At the higher latitudes the satellite will actually be within radio range of a given point on several sequential orbits. As a result, the satellite could provide the location of a polar bear every two hours for half a day. For the other half, the bear would be out of communication.

No polar bear has actually been fitted with a transmitter, however, because some technological problems remain to be overcome. Most electrical batteries cannot produce enough current to operate a transmitter at the low temperatures of the polar bear environment. Moreover, the equipment must be able to withstand frequent immersions as the bear goes in and out of the water. It nonetheless seems probable that these difficulties will be overcome before long, so that polar bears can be equipped to communicate with a satellite.

After spending an arduous day struggling with techniques that yield little information, the Fish and Game Commission biologist dreams of the day satellites will relay all the needed information on polar bears to his office.

A female polar bear and her two white cubs have been out of their den for three weeks. The cubs, now in their second year, are quite easily distinguished from smaller, newborn bears. The mother-bear and her male cub are almost the same size. But, regardless of the bears' size, an educated observer would be able to recognize the clumsy, juvenile movements of the cub, yet to be tempered by years of sealing experience.

Wandering in circles near the coast, the two cubs have been impatiently waiting for their mother to lead them back to their summer sealing grounds. For some reason unknown to them, the she-bear seems reluctant to leave Shugliak this spring.

Following behind the trio, a he-bear tracks the rutting female. Quickly overtaking the family, the he-bear eases closer and closer to the mother-bear. Torn between her cubs and the overwhelming desire to mate, the she-bear leaves them and joins the he-bear. Both cubs, wanting to follow their mother, are discouraged by the great he-bear's growls.

The breakup of the polar bear family varies with each individual group. Many of the families split up when the cubs reach the age of sixteen months. At this time the mother pairs with a he-bear for the purpose of mating. With their mother gone, the cubs often stay together for a short time. Other families will reunite after their mother has mated. Often, these cubs are still suckling and will remain with their mother until the end of the summer. At this time their mother will leave them to prepare a den for her new litter.

MAY
UPERNARK—The Early
Days of Spring

Above Shugliak Island the sky is a piercing blue. The day's clouds have yet to form. From the north the wind begins slowly, builds and blows for three days. Past the band of ice surrounding the island, the wind is pushing the loose floes farther and farther out to sea.

For the first time this year the sun is just beginning to warm the island. Toward the end of May the days will reach fifty warm degrees. The snow-hidden ice dens of the seals begin to melt, forcing the seals to leave their homes and slip into the water.

In the warm May days the first thaw will send drops of water streaming past the snowdrifts. The streams will flow to the frozen rivers and fjords. Great pools of water will settle in the depressions on the ice, creating lakes connected by small streams, eventually trickling into the sea.

With the month's high tides and strong winds, the captured coastal floes are gently released from their winter moorings and ease out to the open sea—for summer sailing.

Beginning late in April and now continuing in the first days of May, the polar bears take great care to catch the departing floes. There will be no bears on Shugliak Island for the next three months. The polar bears float out to catch their favorite food, the seal. If the bears are stranded on the island during summer, they will have a difficult time replenishing their depleted layers of blubber, needed to warm them through the next winter.

On a frozen bay a few miles from Cape Comfort, Little Cub, his mother, and his sister are still searching for the dens of Oogjook seals. On a hill overlooking the bay an Eskimo scans the surrounding area, looking for seals sleeping on the ice. Using a telescope, one passed down to him by his father, he finds the three bears trying to sniff out a seal birth chamber.

He runs back to his komatik, turns the sled around, and drives his dogs down the backslide of the hill, hidden from the bears' view. Using a circular route, the Eskimo attempts to cut off the bears' escape route to the sea, but at the same time stays downwind of the animals.

Just as he reaches the edge of the bay, Little Cub's mother sees the Eskimo's komatik trying to block their escape route. The cubs' mother leads them away from the hunter, running toward the edge of the ice, to the protective sea. The cubs are not capable of running as fast as their mother, and the two quickly fall behind. Their mother waits for them to catch up, then she follows behind them. Once they begin to slow from exhaustion, the big she-bear places her snout under the cubs' haunches and flips them ahead with a good push.

As soon as the huskies are cut loose, they rush to catch up with the three bears. The mother, seeing the huskies close behind, turns and tries to give her cubs an opportunity to escape by making a stand. Unaware of their mother's good intentions, the two cubs wait for her.

Fired by her maternal instinct to protect the cubs and escape the danger, the mother-bear savagely attacks the huskies.

With a great swing of her big paw, she hits a dog and sends it flying. Now that some of the dogs have moved to attack the cubs, Little Cub's mother runs to their rescue. When a dog gets in her way, she quickly dispatches it with her paw.

Now, not far from the open water, the she-bear uses the opportunity to try to escape. Pushing the cubs along beneath her, roaring loudly, and intimidating the dogs with her swinging paw, she is able to reach the water.

Once the three are in the water, the mother grabs first one, then the other cub by the back of the neck and snaps her head back, flipping each cub up on her back. With both cubs on her back, she swims between the floes, away from the land-locked ice.

The Eskimo, finally reaching the point where the bears entered the water, cannot get a good shot at them. With two of his dogs dead and one injured, his hunt for the bears ends in defeat.

Once the bears are far enough from the danger, Little Cub's mother chooses an ice floe and pulls herself and the cubs up on the floating platform. Exhausted from the chase, the she-bear finds a protected ridge of ice to sleep under and warms her chilled cubs.

Little Cub's father is also on his way to the sea to spend his summer on the ice floes. Reaching the land-locked rim of ice, hungry once again, he begins to hunt for the birth chambers of the Oogjook seals. The seal pups must wait until they have grown their thick water-repellent fur before they can enter the water. On the ice they are easy prey for the great he-bear.

After traveling only a few hundred yards, Little Cub's father scents out a seal birth chamber. With the warm spring weather, the massive he-bear has no trouble breaking into the ice-covered den, using his paw. He digs into the den with his snout, picks up the pup with his mouth, and flips it up high in the air. The he-bear walks over to where it lands and begins to roll the bellowing, protesting pup around the ice like a soccer ball. Tired of this game, the bear knocks the pup so hard it slides across the ice, half dead. With a quick snap, the he-bear breaks the pup's neck and begins his meal.

Once Little Cub's father has finished eating his meal, he will look for an appropriate sleeping area for his nap. He takes time out from his search to stop at a pool of water to drink. On the surface of the ice, fresh water accumulates from melting ice and snow. Before he decides on a specific site to sleep, the he-bear will often climb a ridge of ice and survey the area for potential danger.

When the he-bear is settled under a wind-protected ridge, the nap begins. During the next five or six hours, the bear will occasionally wake, lift his head, scan the area with his eyes, and sniff. Once he is satisfied there are no problems, he goes back to sleep. Every so often he will rise, move a few feet, then lie down again to continue his sleep in a new bed.

As Shugliak Island slowly warms, Little Cub's father begins to lose some of his winter coat. Across his muzzle, down his forelegs, and on his belly, the massive he-bear begins to molt. Very soon a large portion of his thick underfur will be shed, leaving large spots, especially on the belly, almost bare. The molting process will linger into August.

Since Little Cub's father has retained a sufficient layer of blubber through the spring, he will not suffer during the summer from lack of protection from the cold. The process of replacement will continue into the autumn until a thick new winter coat is ready to protect the bear against next winter's bitter cold.

An old freighter, flying the flag of Denmark, slowly departs from the harbor of Reykjavik, Iceland. Following the coast northward, the *Horsens* begins a short voyage to the uninhabited shores of Greenland.

In the steering house Captain Römö and his first mate Kath grumble over their foolish voyage. Usually a jolly, rotund man, the captain has nothing good to say about this crazy mission to collect polar bears for American zoos.

"If this was my ship," mutters the first mate, "we would never waste a minute on such stupidity."

In their cabin the two men from Wildlife Enterprises, Inc., discuss their strategy. With orders to collect two young polar bears, they decide on capturing four young cubs. Both men can easily remember the difficulty they had on the last expedition—halfway to New York, three of the four bears they had captured died of a mysterious, unexplainable disease. The memory of three irate customers have made them decide to catch a few extra—just to be on the safe side.

Carefully making their way through the floes and icebergs, they sail past Knud Rasmussen Land, across Scoresby Sound, and to their destination, Jameson Land.

The two hunters are informed of the ship's arrival. Before the excursion boat is lowered, the needed gear is stowed in the bow of the small craft. Once lowered onto the water, they head toward the shore. One of the ship's mates navigates, while the other two attempt to sight a female with her cubs.

Once they reach the land, they set up a small burner and roast strips of seal fat. Catching the scent of the burning blubber, a mother and her two cubs rush toward the irresistible smell. The three men, hiding behind a large block of ice, wait for the three bears to come close enough for them to shoot the mother-bear with a syringe gun. Most men would not bother with tranquilizers—a rifle shot is much easier and safer. Roaring at the now obvious intruders, the she-bear tries to defend her cubs. Once she is shot with the syringe, the tranquilizer slowly takes effect, incapacitating her.

The cubs bellow at their mother's side, but are bound in heavy nets and carried to the waiting boat. As soon as the boat has returned to the ship, the cubs are placed in small iron cages

—their quarters for the rest of the voyage. The three men set out again to capture the third and fourth cubs.

Five hours later the mother polar bear is finally able to stand again. Confused by the tranquilizer, she stumbles around, trying to find her two cubs. Sniffing at the capture site, the cubs' and the vaguely remembered captors' scent are muddled into a puzzle she will never solve. For days the she-bear will seek her abducted cubs.

Back aboard ship, the four cages are now filled. The ship turns to the south and begins its long voyage to New York.

> On a whaling cruise some years before, a mate on a returning homeward voyage had captured a polar bear cub, the dam being killed. The robe was stripped from the mother and placed in the bottom of a large cask, and in this the cub was imprisoned, the staves being bored full of auger holes for ventilation and the cask lashed to a convenient part of the deck. During a fearful storm, it broke loose from its fastenings and brought up against something that broke in one of the heads, and the cub escaped on the deck. The sailors took to the riggings, the cook deserted the captain's flapjacks, and even the helmsman left the wheel to look after itself; and it was some time before Bruin, Jr., could be persuaded to relinquish command by a bullet through his brain.

Now past Cape Farewell, the southern tip of Greenland, one of the cubs becomes sick. For three days everything they feed him is regurgitated. Special formulas, vitamins, and units of antibiotics fail to help him. The night after they sight the Newfoundland coast, the cub dies and is buried at sea.

Both men now watch the other cubs carefully. Fearful of losing the others, they mother the cubs as best they can.

The *Horsens* churns into New York harbor, past the Statue of Liberty, there to be met by a small fleet of tugs. Brought to the special customs dock, the three polar bear cubs are lifted off the ship and set on the wharf. The forklift hauls the cages to a special building for processing. Relieved of the bears and the two men, the captain has the signed delivery papers and can now deliver the remainder of his cargo.

It has been estimated that there are more than one thousand polar bears in the zoos around the world. The demand for live polar bears never stops. Captors are able to get twenty-five hundred dollars plus the cost of transportation for each cub. Between the time the cubs are captured and the time they finally reach their destination, 50 per cent of the cubs die.

The solution to the problem of cost and mortality is obvious. Zoos should make greater efforts to breed their own cubs, saving the wild population from unnecessary pressures. Often it is easier and cheaper to order wild cubs from suppliers instead of setting up the proper facilities to breed previously captured animals. We need a revolution in the minds of zookeepers. They must take the initiative to breed the animals they do have instead of robbing the wild population of their indispensable members.

At the United States Customs quarantine building, a truck backs up to the loading dock. Once the truck is positioned, the two men jump out of the truck and present the necessary papers. A cage is brought out with a forklift, and one of the polar bear cubs is loaded into the truck.

The two men drive off and begin their trip back to their Midwestern zoo. In the back of the truck the cub is uncomfortable in the muggy heat, and the bumps make him dizzy. For twenty-four hours he is bounced around in the cage until they finally reach the zoo. He is lowered into the rock grotto, the cage is opened, and he staggers into his home, where he is to live for the rest of his life.

Little Cub, his mother, and his sister continue their odyssey across the moving ice pack. For the first time, at the age of six months, the cubs will swim unassisted from one floe to another. Their mother, leading the way, swims across the channel between floes. After pulling herself up from the water, she patiently waits for the cubs to finish their swim to the edge of the floe. Once they have reached the floe, she then helps them up the icy, vertical side to the top surface.

Climbing to the top of a ridge of ice, the great she-bear finds a well-protected vantage point for the two cubs to view her hunting techniques. Little Cub's mother, freed of the cubs, begins to hunt for seals basking in the sun. Both cubs watch every move their mother makes. Moving up and down the ice, the she-bear searches for the seal's musky scent.

Bored by their mother's lack of success, the two cubs can no longer contain their mischievousness. As they wrestle together in their hideout, the two cubs accidentally slip down the side of the ice ridge, tumbling to the bottom. Thrilled with their newfound sliding slope, the cubs climb back to the top and carefully slide down. Again and again they slide and roll from the top and then race up to try it once more.

Seeing the cubs from a distance playing on the ice, their mother, annoyed at them for leaving their hideout, lumbers toward them. Absorbed in their play, the cubs fail to notice her approach. Halfway down the slope, they see their mother waiting at the bottom. Tumbling at her feet, Little Cub is the first to be smacked with his mother's paw and rolled over on the ice. His sister receives the same treatment and joins her brother, flat on the ice. After receiving their punishment, the two cubs follow their mother obediently while she resumes her hunt.

Many of the world's mammals claim a specific area in their range as their home territory. This area often includes a denning site and hunting grounds that are preempted and defended by the male of the species. The polar bear does not appear to have a home territory. Due to the rigors of the Arctic winter and other environmental factors, its primary source of food, the seal, is not found in one place consistently for extended periods of time, allowing the establishment of a home territory.

Polar bears have long relied on drifting ice floes as vehicles of movement and hunting platforms. Occasionally, while they sail these icy skiffs, currents have sent them far outside the boundaries of their normal range. Northern currents, winding their way past the coast of Newfoundland, have been known to trap unsuspecting bears, bringing them through Belle Isle Strait and stranding them in the Gulf of St. Lawrence. Most often these unexpected visitors arrive in April and May. Reports from the vicinity of the Gulf of St. Lawrence, hidden in small-town newspapers and scientific journals, tell only of the hunter and the beautiful bear he has killed—far off course.

One record tells of a polar bear being stranded in the Gulf of St. Lawrence in this manner. Tidal currents have been credited with pushing the floating bear farther west, finally depositing him on the northern coast of the Gulf. Continuing his voyage on land, the bear followed the shore of the Gulf of St. Lawrence, turning inland at the Saguenay River. One hundred miles from the Gulf, the bear was finally killed at Lake St. John, the hunter totally perplexed by the location of his unusual victim.

If we asked ourselves where this polar bear was going, a quick investigation using a map of Canada would reveal the answer. The currents flowing past the Newfoundland coast, the same ones that brought the bear south, will prevent him from a return voyage north. The only way for the animal to return home would be overland. If one were to plot the most logical course for the returning bear to follow on his way back to James Bay and Hudson Bay, the Saguenay River route would most likely be chosen. Polar bears do have homing instinct, that remarkable ability to navigate through their environment. There is little question that this is what our wandering bear was doing—returning home on the shortest overland route north.

Somewhere in time between here and Olduvai Gorge,

man has lost his ability to home in on a central point in his environment. In view of the surroundings of the polar bear—vast areas of snow-covered land, long winter nights, and fields of identically appearing ice floes—this ability to navigate is essential to prevent him from becoming lost. Extreme cases, as illustrated by the traveling bear shot at Lake St. John, accent this instinct. Polar bears which have appeared to be lost have surprised many a polar explorer and traveler by crossing islands, neck of land, and expansive peninsulas at the most convenient and advantageous points.

The two white cubs have been alone together exactly one month. After their mother paired with a male, the two second-year cubs have been hunting together and sharing the food they have captured. Just as during their first summer together with their mother, they play together—wrestling, chasing each other, and sliding down ridges of ice. At times the wrestling turns into more than cubs' play—it is almost like adult warfare. Prompted by these accidental incidents, an alarm that has been ticking away for eighteen months runs through both of them. It is time to separate. Their days of being cubs are over. Without emotion, they both depart, now to begin their solitary life as adult polar bears.

JUNE
OOPUNGAKSHUK—
The Days of the
Returning Birds

It is now the month of June in the year of the polar bear. On Shugliak Island it is Oopungakshuk, the season of the returning birds. Even though it is a month of melting snow and sinking snowdrifts, dark clouds occasionally drop a heavy load of snow, leaving new snowbanks.

Above the island during storm-free days, loons fly circular patterns, awaiting the breakup of the frozen lakes. Impatiently they attempt to glide into the lake's spring puddles, only to find that they are still frozen.

Across the snow-covered tundra a hazy fog rises from the melting snow. Jaegers, owls, and gulls bolt through the haze, there to gorge themselves on lemmings running on the ground, flooded out of their tunnels. Foxes, hares, and weasels lose their winter white, turning gray and brown for summer hiding.

Moving across the drifting pack ice, Little Cub, his mother, and his sister continue their search for the seal. Once an ice floe or berg has been thoroughly searched, the bears move to another platform. Sliding into the water, the three swim to the next floe. With their heads low, one cub on each side of their mother, they swim through the water, leaving a trail of ripples across the calm surface. If the swim is long or difficult, the cubs tire. They seize their mother's tail with their teeth and hold on tightly, and the great she-bear tows her cubs to the next floe. Once they have reached the floe, the mother-bear pulls herself up on the surface. Then she grabs the cubs by the back of the neck, lifts them out of the water, and places them next to her on the ice.

An uncle of Little Cub awakes from his sleep. During April the he-bear, having found the carcass of a walrus on Bear Island, ignored the ice floe's retreat from the island. Now he has been isolated for the remainder of the summer; he is too far from other islands or ice floes to swim from his prison. He must wait two months longer before the northern winds drive ice floes to the south, finally releasing him.

There are numerous islands throughout the Arctic seas that have been named Bear Island. Invariably these islands harbor polar bears stranded from the ice pack. Unable to hunt for seals, they must satisfy their hunger with mosses, mushrooms, lichens, and the other varieties of sparse vegetation. If there is more than one bear on an island, it is not uncommon for the stronger of the animals to be forced into cannibalism to survive the summer.

Polar bears are easy prey during their summer stay on these small, rocky islands. Hunters have long timed their arrival in polar regions to coincide with the bear's imprisonment, making their task even easier.

Interested in studying the ecology of the Arctic regions, the American Institute of Biological Sciences sponsored an expedition to the Svalbard Islands during the summer of 1962. Most of the expedition's work was concerned with gathering preliminary information in order to plan long-term studies on the behavior and ecology of the polar bear.

Aboard a chartered sealing vessel, their journey began in July, sailing from the port of Tromsö in northern Norway. The distinguished members of the expedition—Decoursey Martin, marine biologist; A. D. Stenger, motion picture photographer; Fred Baldwin, still photographer; F. M. Hart and Martin Schein of Penn State University—were able to film the swimming techniques of the polar bear.

The members of the group decided that the best method was first to capture a bear, using a tranquilizing gun, and then releasing the bear in an open area. Dr. Schein describes the adventure of photographing the polar bear underwater:

> Since the bear was housed in the cage that was designed to protect the underwater photographer from swimming bears, some degree of coordinated manipulations was in order. First, we selected an ice-free body of rather calm water as the site of operation: "ice-free" so that the bear could not escape, "calm" to aid in photography. The cage plus bear was lowered over the side of the ship and the bear released into the water, where the small boat was waiting to ride herd from a safe, unexcitable distance. Next, the empty cage was raised, and the photographer in his diving suit got in. The cage (plus photographer) was then lowered, and photos were taken as the small boat kept the bear in the vicinity of the cage. When the photographer was finished, the cage was raised and he was released. Then the cage was lowered again, with the door open. Stenger, who happens to be from Texas, lassoed the bear in the water and it was guided back into the cage. The door was closed, after which the cage plus bear was raised and again settled on the deck. The net result of the whole operation, besides getting our pictures, was a desperately needed cleaning.
>
> We were able to repeat the procedure one more

time before the bear escaped from the cage during a storm. She crawled through the hastily wired-over top, roamed the deck for a few minutes, and jumped over the side. She was last seen disappearing into the gloom of a nasty snowstorm. The water was too rough to consider giving chase with the small boat, and besides we felt we had gotten enough information from her. She had earned her freedom.

Its swimming movements were interesting and characteristic; only the front paws are used to paddle, while the hind paws extend rigidly behind and act as a rudder. However, in making a sudden turnabout, the bear rears up by paddling all four legs and then sets off anew. Of interest was this bear's peculiar habit of diving every few minutes or so while swimming, as if the diving were part of its escape mechanism. The dives were of short duration and the bear was at the surface again in five or ten seconds. No other bear that we observed dived in this fashion, but then no other bear was as reluctant to come out of the water. We tried to bait the bear with bits of seal blubber placed on several small floes, but by and large, these were at first ignored. After several hours of escape-type behavior, the bear was visibly tired and did take a few chunks of blubber as it loped across the ice. It also paused long enough in its run to drink fresh water from pools of melted ice on the surface of the floe.

The bear's relationship to the moving edge of the ice pack is coincidental: actually, they are largely confined to the ice pack by their favorite food item, the seals. Since bears are not agile enough to catch seals in the open water, their only hope for a meal is to trap a seal that is resting on the ice. As the ice pack recedes northward in late spring and summer, some bears are stranded on small islands in the area. Although they certainly are capable of swimming many miles at a time, we believe that they normally avoid wide expanses of open water unless there is land or an ice floe in sight. Thus, an ice pack hastened northward by a strong, warm southerly wind could quickly leave a sleeping bear stranded unless it happened to be riding north with the ice.

Contending with severe ice conditions, swimming in frigid Arctic waters, and having their sealing vessel caught and stranded in the ice pack for several days, these men persevered through difficult days in order to capture photograph sequences that are considered to be classics in polar bear research.

Although polar bears are obviously not as well adapted for swimming as many marine mammals or fish, they do possess a number of evolved characteristics that serve them well in the water. The forepaws, larger than the hind paws, have webbing halfway down the length of the toes, giving them greater surface area for paddling. The thick covering of blubber insulates the bears in the water just as it does in the outside air. Their oily skin and hair keep the penetrating cold water from chilling, and also act as waterproofing, making it easy for them to rid their hair of water once they are on land again. The polar bear's great strength and stamina are a great help in propelling him through the water.

Polar bears have been clocked in the water—males swimming one hundred yards in thirty to thirty-three seconds, and she-bears with cubs finishing the same distance in forty seconds. The only type of boat that is capable of catching a he-bear in the drifting ice is a kayak, or a small boat with strong, proficient oarsmen.

Polar bears have a variety of methods for entering the water. Some range from a graceful dive, allowing them to slip easily into the water, to tremendous water-spraying belly flops. Once the bear is in the water, his strong swimming strokes propel him forcibly.

Particularly during the summer months when the drifting pack ice is spread over wide expanses, the polar bear must swim great distances in order to satisfy his vast hunger. Polar bears have been known to swim between fifteen and twenty-five miles to an ice floe, berg, or island, hoping to find seals. If the waves are high and rough, the bears will swim below the surface, breaking water only to breathe. In extraordinary circumstances, it would be conceivable that seventy-five to one hundred miles could be covered in the length of one day by a swimming polar bear.

Though the polar bear is a powerful swimmer, he would much prefer to spend his summer months on drifting ice floes. Where exactly do Little Cub's family and the other inhabitants of Shugliak Island go? For many years the most popular, yet untested theory held that polar bears drifted from one Arctic sea to another. Since the ice pack generally drifts in a clockwise fashion around the pole, it was thought the bears would begin, for example, in the Soviet Arctic, pass Greenland, and eventually end their travels in Baffin Bay, there probably to continue back to the Soviet Arctic through the northern Canadian Islands and past Alaska.

Once research biologists began studying denning and other aspects of the polar bear's life, it was found that relatively the same number of bears would be present in the Hudson Bay region and at other denning sites after summer drifting. If circumpolar drifting was the explanation, what a coincidence that relatively the same number of bears as the year before should return.

We would concur that polar bears on Shugliak Island probably travel the currents only in Foxe Basin, Hudson Bay, and Hudson Strait. By using the currents to drift, they would be able to navigate and return to their home island in the autumn. Suppose a bear were to drift too far from his island or needed ice floes? Swimming could always be used to help him return. Overland travel has never been avoided when absolutely necessary. Some day radio tracking will tell us exactly where polar bears in different parts of the world do travel.

Writing in *True Bear Stories,* Joaquin Miller describes a polar bear's attempt to capture an elusive seal:

> I once saw it watch a seal for half a day, the seal continually escaping, just as the bear was about putting his foot on it, at the escape hole in the ice. Finally it tried to circumvent its prey in another maneuver. It swam off to a distance, and when the seal was again half asleep (at its atluk—escape hole), the bear swam under the ice, with a view to cut off its retreat. It failed, however, and the seal finally escaped. The rage of the animal was boundless, it moaned hideously, tossing the snow in the air, and at last trotted off in a most indignant state of mind.

High in the Canadian Arctic, Jeff Stajich, a young research botanist, concentrates on finding and collecting different species of northern lichens and mosses. He begins his study at the mouth of Peel River and works his way east along Mackenzie Bay. Absorbed in his work, he is too busy to notice where he is going, and he trips over something, falling flat in the mushy tundra. Looking back, he finds an old, white weather-beaten skull. Amused by this strange, prehistoric-looking skull, he stuffs it into his backpack and continues his search for new specimens.

Around their campfire later that same evening, he presents the skull to his companion, a zoologist. The zoologist immediately identifies it as the skull of a polar bear and finds his kit of tools to examine the specimen. From the appearance, he estimates that it has been bleaching in the sun for a minimum of five years. It is unusually well preserved; even the lower jaw is present. With a pair of calipers he measures the length of the maxillary and mandibular molar rows. Comparing these measurements with the results of an earlier study, he finds that the molar rows are considered to be "long," which indicates that this is the skull of a male. Judging from other measurements, he estimates that the bear's weight probably ranged anywhere from eight to nine hundred pounds—a full-grown male. Once they return to the laboratory, he will determine the animal's age by counting rings in its teeth; now he packs their prized specimen for safekeeping.

On ice floes in the distance, a she-bear and her cub can be seen searching for the scent of seals. On the mother's flank, the large number 38 can be seen, the numerals painted by the team of research biologists. Both mother and cub have been prospering in the waters of the Canadian Arctic—for them, summer sealing has been good.

The she-bear, seeing a seal basking in the sun, hides her cub under a protective slab of ice. Sneaking across the ice floe in the shadows, the bear moves closer and closer to the seal. Quietly walking on the hair-covered soles of her feet, the polar bear moves to within fifteen feet of the seal. Now that she is so close, she leaps at the seal in a single agile bound with her forelegs stretched forward, looking very much like a lion striking her prey on the African savannas.

The she-bear immediately falls on the seal and kills it with her left paw. She drags the carcass away from the open water to prevent it from falling in the ocean; then she collects her cub from his hiding spot. Returning to the dead seal, she begins her well-earned meal. The cub eats only a small portion of the blubber, then crawls beneath his mother and finds her breast, there to suck her warm milk.

Stefansson wrote:

A seal does not crawl unguardedly out on the ice; he is always fearful of polar bears. When he wants to come and bask, he spies out the situation by bobbing up from the water as high as he can, lifting his head a foot or two above the general ice-level. This he does at intervals for some time, perhaps for hours, until he concludes there are no bears around and ventures to hitch himself out on the ice.

Here follows another period of extreme vigilance during which the seal lies beside his hole ready to dive in again at the slightest alarm. Eventually, however, he begins to take the naps that were his desire in coming out of the water. But his sleep is restless through fear of bears. He takes naps of thirty or forty or fifty seconds or perhaps a minute. Then he raises his head ten or eighteen inches from the ice and spends five to twenty seconds in making a complete survey of the horizon before taking another nap.

After feasting on the seal's blubber, the mother and her cub set off to find another ice floe. They swim together to a small floe. The she-bear scrambles onto the top surface, then helps her cub up. In a playful mood the she-bear begins to rock the small float back and forth. Sending small waves from both sides of the floe, the she-bear continues her shenanigans, to the delight of her cub.

The polar bear's visual world is marked by intense, glaring sunlight, contrasted by long, dark polar nights. Days are often punctuated with blizzards, sleet, and the constant, driving wind. With these factors present, the bear's vision is rarely given optimum conditions to view his surroundings. When traveling on the ice during good conditions, polar bears are able to identify immobile objects lying on the ice as far as one mile away.

Worth noting is an incident recorded in a whaler's journal. While stranded in Mackenzie Bay, the crew members were participating in one of their time-passing baseball games. As they were playing, a blind polar bear walked through their icy infield. From the appearance of the bear's eyes, the men surmised that the bear had been blind for a considerable period of time. Even though the bear was blind, he was still fat, indicating that he hunted successfully, using only his hearing and smelling senses.

Protected by a glass display case in the Canadian Cultural Museum at Ottawa, an Eskimo ivory carving depicts a polar bear carrying a block of ice on his shoulder while walking on his hind legs. An old Eskimo tale tells of the polar bear swimming carefully toward a large ice floe on which two walruses were sleeping with their calves. The great bear, hidden behind a ridge of ice, picks up a large block of ice with his forepaws. He carries the block on his shoulder, steadying it with his paw and snout.

The bear walks on his hind legs to where the walruses lie. He releases the block from his shoulder, dropping it with great force on the head of a cow, killing it instantly. The other cow and her calf roll into the ocean, safe from the bear. With the walrus mother dead, the calf remains at her side, there to be dispatched by the polar bear.

With the Eskimo's reputation for telling tall tales, it is easy to be skeptical about this story. But other Arctic travelers have observed this same type of polar bear behavior, verifying the Eskimo's story.

A similar variation describes the walrus lying on the rocky shoreline. Seeing the walrus basking in the sun, the polar bear quietly scales a nearby cliff and throws a large rock down on the walrus's head. If the walrus is not killed instantly, the polar bear will charge down from the cliff and, using the same rock, hammer the head of the walrus until it is dead.

The walrus is a bottom feeder, requiring areas with drifting sea ice and strong currents that keep the water sufficiently open. Submerging for ten minutes at one time, the walrus reaches the sand or mud banks as deep as 250 feet below the surface. On the bottom the walrus uses his long ivory tusks to rake through the ocean floor, digging up sea snails, sand worms, starfish, sea-urchins, shrimp, clams, cockles, and mussels.

The polar bear and walrus, traditional rivals, occasionally come in contact while feeding on whale carcasses or while killing seals. If a walrus is in the water, a polar bear will not enter. The walrus is the only polar animal that the bear really fears.

Reaching fifteen feet in length and weighing as much as one and a half tons, the walrus is more than a formidable adversary. If the two animals encounter each other on land, the polar bear will have an edge. When they meet each other in the water, the walrus has been known to grab the polar bear from below and, using his ivory tusks, which often grow more than thirty inches in length, to stab the bear in the back, driving the tusks to the hilt. The carcasses of polar bears and walruses have been found coupled in this manner.

Beechey describes an encounter he observed, while living in Spitsbergen, between a polar bear and a walrus:

> [A walrus] rose in a pool of water not very far from us and, after looking around, drew his greasy carcass upon the ice, where he rolled about for a time, and at length laid himself down to sleep. A bear, which had probably been observing his movements, crawled carefully upon the ice on the opposite side of the pool, and began to roll about also, but apparently more with design than amusement, as he progressively lessened the distance that intervened between him and his prey. The walrus, suspicious of his advances, drew himself up, preparatory to precipitate retreat into the water, in case of a nearer acquaintance with this playful but treacherous visitor; on which the bear was instantly motionless, as if in the act of sleep; but after a time began to lick his paws and clean himself, and occasionally to encroach a little more upon his intended prey. But even this artifice did not succeed; the wary walrus was far too cunning to

allow himself to be entrapped, and suddenly plunged into the pool; which the bear no sooner observed than he threw off all disguise, rushed toward the spot, and followed him in an instant into the water, where I fear he was as much disappointed in his meal as we were of the pleasure of witnessing a very interesting encounter.

Little Cub's father, many miles from land, is floating on the drifting pack ice, hunting for seals. Walking along channels of open water, he searches for the young seals surfacing to breathe. With their young lungs yet unaccustomed to deep dives, they must surface three times as often as their adult parents. Breaking the surface so often leaves them unprotected and easy prey for the polar bear.

Little Cub's father, tired of walking across the drifting ice floes, finally lies down on the edge of the ice. The great he-bear begins to watch for seals swimming in the leads of open water. His conspicuous nose covered with his forepaw, the stalking bear's head must look, to the submerged seals, like just another piece of ice hanging over the water. Like almost every other wait in the Arctic, it lasts a long time.

Suddenly a seal appears, breaking the surface of the water. At first the seal swims back and forth, yards from the crouching bear. Muscles tensed, ready to spring, the bear waits. Swimming closer and closer, the seal breathes deeply of the cool air, anticipating his next dive. Afraid this chance is his last, the bear springs at the seal, but his claw merely grazes the seal's slick coat, and the seal dives to safety.

The bear paddles back to the edge of the ice, pulls himself up, and shakes his coat. Turning to the rippled surface, the great he-bear repeatedly hits the water with his paw, sending up walls of it. His anger unabated, he turns, tosses snow in the air, and roars horribly at his unfortunate luck.

JULY
MITTIADLUT—
The Season of Warmth

Suddenly fog-covered Shugliak Island has changed colors —has transformed itself from snowy white to shades of yellow, brown, and even hints of green. Summer has forced out the leaves of the cold-crippled willow and birch trees, renegades far above the limits of the northern tree line. The stunted purple, white, and golden Arctic flowers decorate the meadows. Bumblebees and butterflies feverishly collect summer's short supply of nectar. Every warm day mosquitoes stream from the marshes to torment the animals across the tundra.

Rejoicing over ice-free lakes, the Arctic loon breaks the long winter silence. Sounding the screech of a dog when his tail or leg has been stepped on, the loon announces his dive as he heads for his summer lake, there to join a bobbing flock of brant geese.

With summer's arrival, there are birds everywhere— plovers, king eider ducks, phalaropes, snowy owls, and white-rumped sandpipers. At dusk tall cranes strut deliberately across the meadows, the ground porous with lemming burrows. The bark of the Arctic fox and the rumbling of roving herds of caribou break the monotonous howl of the wind.

It is mid-July before the ice is broken out of well-protected bays. Although much of the snow has already melted, white flakes may fall during any one of the summer days.

Living on the drifting pack ice, Little Cub has grown quickly during the late spring and summer. He now weighs more than 130 pounds and is almost four feet in length. He has gone through his first molt, losing much of his infant hair, and now his thickened, coarser adult hair has begun to grow.

For Little Cub's mother, it has been a good spring for capturing seals. She and her cubs have feasted often. Both cubs have slowly grown to like the fishy-tasting seal's blubber, eating more than four pounds of it at each meal.

With their diet turning toward seal blubber, they are slowly losing interest in suckling at their mother's breast. Depending on the supply of food, the cubs will be able to survive without the milk. If there is little seal blubber to eat, the cubs will rely more on the milk. Many cubs who have found it difficult to get food have continued to nurse as long as twelve to sixteen months.

For two months Little Cub and his family have not visited any of the islands or the mainland in the region—they have remained on the drifting ice floes. Little Cub's mother, anticipating their eventual breakup, has spent most of this time giving her cubs lessons in the art of hunting seals.

During the summer months seals spend much of their time lying on ice floes, basking in the sun. Polar bears will seize this opportunity to surprise the seals.

Roaming over a large floe, the three bears spot a seal lying next to the ocean. The hunting party, walking directly into the breeze, moves through shadows and behind protective ice shields to within thirty feet of the seal.

Little Cub is allowed to take the lead by his mother. Even though she is directly behind him, it is Little Cub's first unassisted attempt at hunting. Moving closer and closer, he begins his running charge too soon. The sleeping seal, startled by the charge, begins his roll into the water. Little Cub, now in mid-air, his target moving, can only tag the seal as it enters the water. Embarrassed by his failure, he watches the seal swim out of sight.

Polar bears have little difficulty dispatching the young and smaller species of seals basking on the ice. Using his massive paw, a he-bear will crush the seal's skull with one blow. If the situation is right, the bear will bite into the seal's vulnerable neck. Occasionally the larger species, such as the hooded seal, will attempt to fight the polar bear. Hooded seals, their head and body measuring eleven feet, their weight as much as nine hundred pounds, will snap at the bear, struggling with every ounce of muscle. A few of the more fortunate seals are able to show scars from their stand-off with the great white bear, but more often than not they are the losers.

Eskimos have often mentioned seeing the rather curious meeting of polar bears and seals while both are swimming in the water. The seal, a proficient swimmer, is accustomed to remaining submerged for twenty minutes and is credited with swimming a hundred yards in ten seconds. Seals can quite literally swim circles around a swimming polar bear.

Just as a seal is defenseless on land, the polar bear leaves himself open to seals' contemptuous attacks while in the water. When ringed seals are in a group of four or six, they will quite daringly swim up to a polar bear and snap at his hindquarters. Although they are not able to do the bear any real injury, the seals can force him to swim to the nearest floating platform or land as fast as he can.

Illingworth wrote:

I witnessed . . . an episode in Ice Fjord, where seals are to be found in fair numbers on the floes floating off the larger glaciers. For some time we watched a bear stalking a seal close inshore where shelf-ice meets the rocks. He took immense pains to advance unseen, but this was not to be his successful day, for as he launched his final rush the seal rolled neatly into the water and was gone. The bear might have retained his equilibrium had the seal had the tact not to raise a grinning head above the water (apparently to see who it was [who] had disturbed its slumber). In a fit of rage the bear smashed his paw against a rock outcrop, breaking every bone in his right paw and severely injuring the left, as was discovered when subsequently the animal was shot.

The temperature variation in the polar bear's world is great—during the winter the thermometer may register as low as 50, 60, even 70 degrees below zero; in summer the temperature may be as high as 80 degrees. Having a number of efficient adaptations designed to save body heat, the polar bear's ability to dissipate heat in warm summer weather limits him to fifteen minutes of hard work on land due to overheating. The bear is able to run away from danger much more easily in winter than in summer.

When Little Cub's mother becomes overheated, there are a number of mechanisms she uses to cool off. Finding a shady place to lie down in, she will extend her limbs to provide maximum body surface contact with the air. Just as dogs and other animals pant in order to cool off, so does Little Cub's mother.

As her body temperature increases, so does her heart rate. Along both sides of her shoulders, between her outer skin and blubber, lie striated muscle sheets, abundantly supplied with an intricate network of blood vessels to act as areas of heat dissipation. The air will cool the blood as it passes so close to the skin.

Photographs by
Bruce Coleman, Inc.

If open water is available, the polar bear will dive in, cooling off in the chilling water.

Little Cub's father climbs onto an ice floe. In his search for seals he has had to swim many miles now that the summer sun has melted much of the ice. Standing on his hind legs, he scans the ice floe for the dark seals bathing in the sun.

He spots a seal on the opposite side of the floe and begins the long approach, directly into the wind. At first he is able to hide behind piles of ice, concealing himself in the shadows. Once he has passed a series of ridges, he has no place to hide. Lying flat on his stomach, he begins to crawl closer and closer to the seal. At first he pushes a small clump of ice and snow in front of him to hide his conspicuous black nose and eyes. His white coat blends in well with the surroundings, making it difficult for the seal to see the he-bear approaching.

When the seal wakes from his sleep and lifts his head, Little Cub's father lies perfectly still, remaining frozen until the seal puts his head down again. Still pushing the ice screen in front of him, the he-bear advances slowly again until he is close enough. Then he springs from his prostrate position, bounds the last few feet to the seal, hurling himself through the air, killing the seal instantly.

It does not occur often, but occasionally a polar bear will not eat the seal he has just killed. This behavior is usually limited to the summer months. Polar bears cannot afford to pass up a meal during the winter, for most of the time they are voraciously hungry. Some biologists have suggested that un-eaten seals are too old, smell rancid, and are therefore unap-petizing to the bear. Others believe the he-bear is just amusing himself with killing.

When seals are abundant and the polar bear is not ex-ceedingly hungry, he eats only the blood and blubber. If seals are difficult to find, the smaller species will be completely consumed by the bear. Usually, at one sitting, the bear will eat from fifteen to fifty pounds of blubber in order to satisfy his hunger. Large polar bears have been killed with more than 150 pounds of blubber in their stomachs. Extraordinarily hungry bears with even eat the seal's bones.

Man's relationship with the polar bear has been mixed with a good measure of prejudice and a small degree of impartial observation. If one is confronted by a polar bear in a personally threatening situation, it is understandable that any curiosity exhibited by the bear will be considered overt aggression.

Man's influence over the years has caused a marked behavioral change in the polar bear. In the southern portions of the polar bear's range, the bears are shy and easily frightened, due to numerous encounters with explorers, whalers, and hunters. In the northern areas bears are much more curious and aggressive. In these regions the polar bear rarely meets man.

Particularly in earlier years when polar travelers and inhabitants first encountered the huge bears, these men were terribly frightened. In many of the descriptions the bear sounds more curious than aggressive. Gerrit de Veer relates one of his many experiences with polar bears:

A beare came bouldly toward the house, and came downe the staires close to the dore, seeking to breake into the house; but our master held the dore fast to, and being in great haste and feare, could not barre it with the peece of wood that we used thereunto, but the beare seeing that the dore was shut, she went backe againe, and within two houres after she came againe, and went round about and upon the top of the house, and made such a roaring that it was fearefull to heare, and at last got to the chimney, and made such worke there that we thought she would have broken it downe, and tore the saile that was made fast about it in many peeces with a great fearefull noise; but for that it was night we made no resistance against her, because we could not see her. At last she went awaie and left us.

Curiosity with the polar bear has led to a number of humorous encounters and to some ending in tragedy. The first story tells of a sailor from the *Germania* expedition, the first to over-winter in northeast Greenland.

He . . . seated himself on a rock, and sang a song in the still air. As he looked behind him, however, he saw, not many steps off, a huge bear, which with great gravity was watching the stranger.

Flight is the only, though a doubtful, chance of safety, and he began to hurry down the mountain. Upon looking back, after a time, he perceived the great bear trotting behind him at a little distance, like a great dog. Thus they descended the mountain for some time. If he halted, so did the bear; when he went on, the bear followed slowly; if he began to run, the bear did the same. At this dreadful moment—and it was most likely his preservation—while running, he pulled off his jacket, throwing it behind him. The bear stops and begins to examine the jacket. The sailor gains courage, rushes on down the mountain, sending out a shout for help, which resounds through the silent region. But soon the bear is again at his heels, and he must throw away cap and waist coat, by which he gains a little. Now he sees help approaching— several friends hurrying over the ice. Collecting his last strength, he shouts and runs on. But help seems in vain, for the pursuer hurries too, and he is obliged to take the last thing he has, his shawl which he throws exactly over the monster's snout, who, more excited still by renewed shouting, throws it back again contemptuously with a toss of the head, and presses forward upon the defenceless man, who feels his cold black snout touch his hand. Fixedly he stared into the merciless eyes of the beast— one short moment of doubt—the bear was startled, his attention seemed drawn aside, and the next moment he was off at a gallop. The shouts of the many hurrying to the rescue had evidently frightened him. From the effects of this day several suffered slightly from pains in the chest and two had large frost-blisters on their feet. No wonder, when they had run about in stockinged feet for a whole hour and a half!

Ernest Seton tells the story of two Eskimos tending their seal nets:

> One incident was related to me which occurred near Point Hope, during the winter of 1880–81. Two men went out from Point Hope during one of the long winter nights, to attend to their seal nets, which were set through holes in the ice. While at work near each other, one of the men heard a Bear approaching over the frosty snow, and having no other weapon but a small knife, the Bear being between him and the shore, he threw himself upon his back upon the ice and waited. The Bear came up in a few moments, and smelled about the man from head to foot, and finally pressed his cold nose against the man's lips and nose, and sniffed several times; each time the terrified Eskimo held his breath until, as he afterwards said, his lungs nearly burst. The Bear suddenly heard the other man at work, and listening for a moment, he started towards him at a gallop, while the man he left sprang to his feet, and ran for his life for the village, and reached it safely. At midday, when the sun had risen a little, a large party went to the spot and found the bear finishing his feast upon the other hunter, and soon dispatching him.

Feigning death and allowing the bear to satisfy his insatiable curiosity is the best defense. Only a few people have the self-control to endure the curious probes of the polar bear. We can only guess how the other man tried to defend himself—quite obviously not as well as the first man.

M'Clintock and Haig-Thomas, both polar travelers, have related similar incidents to Seton's:

> He [a native of Upernivik] found a seal entangled and whilst kneeling down over it upon the ice to get it clear, he received a slap on the back—from his companion as he supposed; but a second and heavier blow made him look smartly round. He was horror-stricken to see a particularly grim old-bear instead of his comrade. Without deigning further notice of the man, Bruin tore the seal out of the net and commenced his supper.

> [A polar bear was] stalking another Eskimo who was bent over an aglo, waiting with raised harpoon for a seal to blow. A strong wind prevented their shouting a warning to the man and they could only watch the bear walk quietly up to him and poke its nose into his back. In this instance, however, the Eskimo's shriek startled the polar bear and they ran off in opposite directions.

Alwin Pederson contends:

> When a male bear sees a man, whether on land or on the ice, its insatiable curiosity always makes it approach. It comes along in its usual amble, without any sign of hurrying, and there is no means of getting out of its way. Every movement or noise excites its curiosity. If one is unarmed and without shelter it seems to me that the best plan is to remain quite still, for it does not necessarily follow that the bear will do you any harm when it does eventually reach you; it may lose interest before it gets to you, or only sniff at you and then move off. I can vouch for this because I once found myself unarmed in the presence of a bear in the following circumstances: The terrain was unsuitable for sledges, and so I had gone on ahead on skis to find a route, and, thinking I would soon return, I had left my gun on the sledge. I had reached the foot of a glacier and was looking for a route when, suddenly, I saw a bear. It did not appear to

have seen me, and so I immediately tried to hide between two blocks of ice at the foot of the steep wall of the glacier. To do this I had to remove my skis; I sank in up to my knees in the snow and was quite immobilized. The bear was ambling along quite peacefully and it still did not appear to have noticed me. When it reached the tracks made by my skis it stopped and sniffed the air. Then for a moment it gazed far away on to the ice. It turned its head and at the same time saw me. The distance between us was exactly five paces. I did not move a muscle. The bear remained watching me for about a minute. I was still quite motionless, but I swear I could hear my heart beating. Then the animal moved off and continued its journey as though I did not exist. I have no doubt that if I had moved at the critical moment, or shouted for help, it would have come at once and the situation would have been very tricky.

Dr. Charles Jonkel, a research scientist with the Canadian Wildlife Service, has studied some of the more recent attacks by the polar bear on man.

In 1966 a boy was attacked near Fort Churchill, Manitoba, Canada. Performing an autopsy on the bear, Dr. Jonkel found a number of interesting and revealing facts. The bear had been wounded by gunshot earlier in the year, causing a canine tooth to be driven into the nasal passage, resulting in blindness in one eye. On the same day before the mauling of the boy, the bear had been wounded in the hind legs and abdomen. The police report, filed after the attack, listed the incident as an unprovoked attack.

In the same area a young Eskimo was killed in 1968 by a polar bear. The boy and a number of his comrades were tracking the bear along the Hudson Bay coast. Advancing too close, they disturbed the bear when he was bedded down. Afraid of being cornered, the bear attacked. No physical impairments were found, but the bear did have garbage in his stomach. Had this group not tracked and disturbed the bear, the Eskimo's death could have been easily avoided.

As more human settlements, mineral explorers, and scientific communities move to the Arctic regions, the polar bear will be confronted with greater frequency. For the first time, these settlements in the Arctic are receiving needed health services and supplies. These changes are allowing local populations to expand faster than ever before, resulting in increased pressures on wildlife populations. Jack Lentfer, of Alaska's Department of Fish and Game, is concerned with the influence of human activity particularly in the polar bear's range. Lentfer writes:

> With the expanding human population and attendant exploitation of natural resources, man will have a greater impact in the Arctic. The most immediate concern with regard to sea ice and polar bears is oil explorations, offshore drilling, and the transport of oil by ships through ice-covered seas.
>
> Oil spills would probably result if wells were drilled offshore and oil were transported by ship. From documentation of oil activity in Cook Inlet in south-central Alaska, it appears that spills would be inevitable. Moving ice would pose a threat to offshore drilling platforms, pumping facilities and transport ships. In the case of a leaking transport ship, ice would hamper or prevent repairs at sea and might delay travel to a docking area. Ice would hinder or prevent a mopping-up or containing of a spill, and currents could spread a large spill over a considerable area. Oil spills would affect polar bears by reducing the insulating value of their fur and adversely affecting species in the food chain below them.

Luring the polar bear with their cooking odors and garbage, humans must learn to be patient with the bears, a virtue not extended to most animals. Dr. Jonkel sums up the basis of the problem by stating:

Polar bears are apparently not looked upon by these people as the "Great White Bear of the North," but rather as creatures akin to rats. Should the present trend continue, this view of polar bears will prevail as it has in regard to the black and grizzly bears in some southern regions.

Little Cub's mother senses the change. Across Foxe Basin the great northeast wind begins to blow. With summer's warm sun, the ice floes have slowly been melting and the drifting pack ice has been receding northward. But now the wind will blow new floes down from the north. The she-bear and her cubs can now begin their return journey to their home island. Having carefully moved across the drifting ice, the three bears are being carried by the currents back to Shugliak Island. With the wind at their back, their trip will soon end and they will be home.

AUGUST
UKIAK—The Days
of Autumn

The warm season fades during the month of August. The green leaves on the scrubby, stunted trees, having grown during the short summer, are just reaching full growth and maturity. Now they begin to turn gold and crimson. The yellow flowers of the poppy have bloomed, hardly opening before they turn into frozen, dried shells.

By the end of August all signs of summer have disappeared. With cool temperatures and the biting frost returning, the ground will soon be ready for autumn's first snowfall. The Arctic hare and many of the other animals have begun their gradual color change. When the first snows cover the ground, these small animals will be well protected with their winter coloration.

In the early days of August the coastal waters around Shugliak Island are almost completely free of the floating, drifting ice—unusual except for this season of the year. As August progresses, the northeasterly winds build up stronger and stronger. Across Foxe Basin, miles of open spaces draw the swift flow of wind. Masses of ice begin moving south with the wind.

Little Cub, his mother, and his sister have been rafting toward their home for one week. This will be the eleventh year Little Cub's mother has navigated through the currents of Foxe Basin to Shugliak Island. The three ride past Melville Peninsula, Winter Island, to the waters of Foxe Channel. Watching closely, Little Cub's mother searches her island's familiar, rugged coastline for the long-awaited landmark.

Sighting the high cliffs of Seahorse Point, the three bears slip into the water and begin the long swim to their home.

For hundreds and perhaps even thousands of years, Seahorse Point has been a landing place for rafting polar bears. Eskimo stories, going back many years, tell of large numbers of polar bears landing at this point during autumn. Crevices and gullies, packed with insulating drifts of snow, attract the denning bears. More recent observations have reported that as many as two hundred bears land on the eastern coast of Shugliak Island during August and September.

From various counts that have been made through the years, the number of bears landing on the island varies each year, depending on the ice conditions. If the summer sun has left few ice floes to be pushed by the northeastern winds, the number of bears will be low. In years when cooler temperatures have prevailed and more ice reaches the island, the polar bear population will be greater.

Scientists have long wondered why pregnant females concentrate in these core denning areas during autumn. Many scientists maintain autumn's annual winds, currents, and tides funnel a large number of the region's drifting polar bears into specific core denning areas. Still, the bears must be aware of their movements and in control to some extent.

After the long swim to Seahorse Point the three bears climb out of the water onto the dry land. They shake their coats free of water and begin the search for food. With many of the ice floes melting in the warm summer sun, the three bears have had difficulty catching seals in the past two weeks. Some of their blubber has been used to sustain them through the poor hunting, and they all look somewhat thin.

In their search for food they will eat almost anything that appears edible. Logs that have been washed up on the beach are gnawed for insects and other invertebrates inside. Mushrooms, mosses, grasses, sedges, and lichens are pulled from the tundra and eaten—a real treat after months of eating only seal blubber.

Just like their Ursidae cousins to the south—the grizzly, big brown, and black bear—Little Cub, his mother, and his sister seek out the berry bushes. The patches of bearberries, crowberries, cranberries, and bilberries will support the bears for weeks. Most bears would prefer the berries to any other vegetation. During August and September it is not uncommon to see polar bears with blue stains around their mouths and on their rump from indulging in gluttonous feasts in bilberry patches. As soon as the first snows fall, many of the berries are frozen and hidden until the following spring.

Polar bears, living in the high Arctic, do not have the same variety of food as the members of their species living in the southern regions of their range. The farther north one goes, the number of species and availability of vegetation are greatly reduced. Consequently the bears must depend on seals and carrion, even during the summer.

When pressed to find food in the summer, polar bears have been known to swim to the sides of ships and beg for scraps of seal blubber. Eskimos and other polar inhabitants have occasionally seen hungry polar bears digging for puffins, the small birds that live in burrow nests in the ground.

Little Cub and his family, foraging on different types of vegetation, slowly progress northward along the eastern coast of Shugliak. With the continued northeastern winds, they are joined by large numbers of other polar bears, all searching for vegetation. Little Cub's mother still takes great care in avoiding confrontations with other bears.

After the polar bears have landed on Shugliak Island in the autumn, behavioral changes occur as they move along the coast and toward inland regions. Many of the bears become restless and belligerent. No doubt the change in their daily habits has much to do with these behavioral outbreaks. Instead of roaming across the drifting ice floes hunting for seals, the bears lead a sedate life on land. Once the bears are able to accustom themselves to a change of diet and surroundings, they progressively become more lethargic. After eating the available vegetation, they dig open pits in the ground and spend a great deal of time sleeping in them.

Little Cub's father arrives on Shugliak Island one week later than his family. The strong winds have delivered him farther to the north, miles above Cape Comfort. Once the great he-bear has walked onto the shore, he immediately catches the putrid odor of rotting flesh and ambles toward the smell. Two miles from his point of landing, the source of the odor lies before him. A sixty-foot bowhead whale had accidentally beached himself. Already a congregation of thirty-seven polar bears has begun to feast on the rotting blubber.

Often the polar bear will exist peacefully at the site of carrion with many members of his own species standing only a few feet away. Any fights taking place are short-lived and infrequently repeated. The strongest bears rule the site of the carrion with quiet authority, the weaker bears avoiding any confrontations. Most bears are content to keep to themselves for the sake of an easy and savory meal.

Polar bears have long relied on carrion in the form of dead whales, seals, walruses, polar bears, and other marine animals. Particularly in August and during the rest of autumn, the search for carrion along the coast is fastidiously thorough.

Eskimos have often noted the presence of polar bears in the vicinity of a walrus carcass; sometimes a bear spends the whole winter near the body. If the carcass yields many meals, the bear will dig a small open pit in the ground and stay nearby, protecting his food supply.

On January 8, 1633, while living on Spitsbergen, Van der Brugge wrote:

> The whole of the day and night we have had so many bears around our tent, making such a terrible noise by their growling, that if it had been continuously night, we would have been in constant fear. The bears kept together in troops—a number gathered round the carcass of a whale; young ones clawing up seaweed or grazing like cattle on the grass; others digging large pits near an unused hut in which to shelter from the wind. When the moon was rising in the evening, parties of three or four or six together could be seen leaving the whale, and passing the hut, growling, presumably on their way to shelter in the hills, for at the end of February the men discovered that they had pitched their camp behind a hill, and made large, deep pits in the ice and snow. They had found there a carcass or tongue of a whale, which they had clawed up out of the ice to the length of a man, and nearly devoured!

Polar bears are not the only animals in search of carrion. Wolves, foxes, ravens, and glaucous gulls wait until they are given the chance to feed. The wolves and foxes often must watch for the last bear to leave the area—if they venture too close before the bears are finished, they may end up being killed by a swipe from the polar bear's paw and devoured.

The Arctic fox has frequently been called the Arctic jackal by northern ecologists. Following the polar bear during the winter, the fox eats the leftovers from the bear's kill. The polar bear laps up the blood and eats only the entrails and blubber, leaving the flesh—skeletal muscles—for the fox.

The Arctic fox measures only twenty inches from nose to rump. At the most he will weigh fifteen pounds. During the summer the fox will concentrate on catching the Arctic lemming and finding carrion. When the polar bear localizes his winter hunting near islands or the mainland, the fox will trail the bear from a safe distance to eat his leftovers and even dig out the undigested matter in the bear's excrement.

Scientists, particularly biologists, have been studying the concentration levels of insecticides throughout the world. The Arctic regions have not been ignored by the insecticides or by the men who study them.

A number of different tissues from the polar bear have made the long journey from the polar regions to laboratories capable of distinguishing the chemicals present. Both DDT and DDT metabolite have been consistently found in the bear's muscle tissues. Unusually high concentration levels of dieldrin, another insecticide, have been detected in the fat tissues of bears.

It is quite easy to follow the path of the insecticides as they climb to the top of the food pyramid. Washing off the land with the fall of rain, these chemicals flow from small streams into rivers and eventually to the ocean. Ocean currents then disperse the chemicals to every ocean, sea, bay, and cove around the world. Invertebrates, filtering through the ocean bottom for nutrients, inadvertently consume the invisible poisons, storing them in their microscopic bodies. Feeding on thousands of these marine invertebrates, seals store the chemicals. With the polar bear eating as many as fifty seals a year, the insecticides move and concentrate at the top of this Arctic food chain.

It is not surprising that high concentrations of these chemicals are detected so far from the fields they were sprayed on. What is surprising is the blasé attitude exhibited by the general populace. DDT and many other insecticides just as harmful are still being used, but no one seems to care.

In the first half of the nineteenth century whaling was a profitable trade in both Hudson Bay and Baffin Bay. Whalers, supplementing their catches, would shoot the abundant polar bears for their meat and pelts. Records of whalers killing more than thirty polar bears in one small cove are not uncommon.

Toward the middle of the nineteenth century the whaling industry was slowly eclipsed by sealing. As this change progressed, more polar bears were killed. In the early years of the twentieth century as many as eight hundred bears a year were claimed by some sealing expeditions.

Lacking weapons that were precision instruments and capable of killing their prey from a safe distance, early polar-bear hunters and Arctic explorers were often stricken with terror at the challenge of the Great White Bear.

Gerrit de Veer, the historian of William Barents's second expedition, wrote in his notes:

> The sixth of September, some of our men went on shore, upon the firme land (Nova Zemlya) to seeke for stones, which are a kinde of diamond, whereof there are many also in the States Island; and while they were seeking the stones, two of our men lying together in one place, a great leane white beare came suddenly stealing out, and caught one of them fast by the necke; cried out and said, "Who is it that pulls me so by the necke?" Wherewith the other, that lay not farre from him, lifted up his head to see who it was; and, perceiving it to be a monsterous beare, cryed out and sayd, "Oh, Mate! it is a beare," and there with presently rose up and ran away. The beare at the first faling upon the man, bit his head in sunder and suckt out his blood; wherewith the rest of the men that were on the land, being about twentie in

number, ran presently thither, either to save the man, or else to drive the beare from the dead body; and having charged their peeces, and bent their pikes, set upon her that still was devouring the man, but, perceiving them to come towards her, fiercely and cruelly ran at them, and gat another of them out from the companie, which she tare in peeces, wherewith all the rest ran away.

We perceiving out of our ship and pinace, that our men ran to the sea—side to save themselves, with all speed entered into our boates, and rowed as fast as we could to the shoare to relieve our men. Where being on land, we beheld the cruell spectacle of our two dead men, that had beene so cruelly killed and torne in pieces by the beare. Wee, seeing that, incouraged our men to goe backe againe with us, and with peeces, curtleaxes, and halfe-pikes to set upon the beare, but they would not all agree thereunto. some of them saying, our men are already dead, and we shall get the beare well enough, though wee oppose not ourselves into so open danger; if wee might save our fellowes' lives, then wee would make haste; but now wee neede not make such speede, but to take her at an advantage, with most securitie for ourselves, for we have to doe with a cruell, fierce, and ravenous beast. Where upon three of our men went forward, the beare still devouring her prey, not once fearing the number of our men, and yet they were thirtie at the least; the three that went forward in that sort Cornelius Jacobson, Wilhelm Geyson and Hans Van Nuflen, Wilhelm Barents' purser; and, after that the sayd maister and pilote had shot three times, and mist, the purser, stepping somewhat further forward, and seeing the beare to be within the length of a shot, shot her into the head, betweene both the eyes, and yet shee held the man still faste by the necke, and lifted up her head, with the man in her mouth; but shee beganne somewhat to stagger; wherewith the purser and a Scottish man drew out their curtleaxes and strooke at her so hard that their curtleaxes burst, and yet she would not leave the man; at last Wilhelm Geyson went to their rescue; and with all his might strooke the beare upon the snout with his peece, at which time the beare fell to the ground, making a great noyse, and Wilhelm Geyson, leaping upon her, cut her throat.

Frederick Schwatka tells of confronting a polar bear wounded during an 1885 hunting expedition:

Not many years ago, the crew of a boat belonging to a ship in the whale-fishery shot at a bear at a little distance, and wounded it. The animal set up a dreadfull howl, and ran along the ice toward the boat. Before he reached it a second shot was fired, which hit him. This served but to increase his fury. He presently swam to the boat, and in attempting to get on board, placed one of his fore feet upon the gunwale; but a sailor having a hatchet in his hand cut it off. The animal, however, still continued to swim after them till they arrived at the ship; but on reaching the ship he immediately ascended the deck; and the crew having fled into the shrouds, he was pursuing them thither when a shot laid him dead on the deck.

SEPTEMBER
OOKUIKSHAK—
Days of the First Snow
and Migrating Birds

For polar bears on Shugliak Island the month of September could correctly be named the month of laziness. Little Cub, his mother, and his sister have excavated a small pit, ten feet in diameter. After occasionally foraging for vegetation, they return to the pit, hidden in a gully near the ocean—there to sleep for most of the month. Hindered by layers of snow covering much of the vegetation, and insufficient numbers of ice floes to serve as sealing platforms, they find it easier to sleep and wait for good ice and sealing conditions.

Little Cub awakes often from his sleep. Gnawing on bits of wood and even on rocks, he tries to ease the pain pulsating from his gums. His permanent dentition is just beginning to break through, and his gums are swollen and inflamed.

In several weeks his teeth will have completely erupted, with the exception of his canines. Little Cub will be three or four years old before his canines are fully developed. Until his teeth have erupted, he must be content with trying to sleep through the pain.

The length of daylight during early September notice-ably shortens. By mid-September the sun will set at the North Pole for the last time this year. It will be a long, dark winter. Below the Arctic Circle on Shugliak Island the sun will rise and set every winter day, even though it just breaks above the horizon on some days.

It is difficult to tell if there is an autumn on Shugliak. Summer turns into winter so quickly that autumn is lost. Snow begins to fall early in September, covering the brown grass and withered plants. Falling lightly at first, it drops into the crevices, gullies, and any protected niche away from the wind. The howl of winter sweeps the tundra of its snow, packing any hidden corner deep and thick. Once again it is turning cold.

With the arrival of the first snows, the birds begin to leave. It is an event one hardly notices. Unexpectedly they are gone until next spring.

Stranded on the northeast coast of Novaya Zemlya with his sixteen men, Barents experienced the severe winter of 1596–1597. As early as September 27, 1596, Gerrit de Veer wrote:

> It frose so hard that as we put a nayle into our mouths (as when men worke carpenters worke they use to doe), there would ice hang thereon when we tooke it out againe, and made the blood follow. The same day there came an old beare and a young one towards us as we were going to our house, beeing altogether (for we durst not go alone), which we thought to shoot at, but she ran away.

Little Cub's father has been eating the berries, grasses, and mushrooms for the past weeks. When not foraging for vegetation, the he-bear sleeps in the natural shelter he has found under a cliff.

Since last May Little Cub's father has been shedding last

winter's heavy coat. During the short summer, clumps of hair have fallen to the ground, leaving his coat looking shaggy. Spurred by September's cold, the dense underfur begins to grow. The outer coat's guard hair will be completely grown out by the last days of October—just in time to protect the he-bear against winter's cold blast.

Today, while searching for berries, he catches the scent of rotting flesh. Walking in a slow, deliberate manner, he makes his way to the edge of the ocean. Floating a few yards from shore is a dead, bloated seal. He wades and swims to the bobbing carcass, grabs the rotting seal with his teeth, and tows the body ashore. He drags it a few feet from the water's edge and stands over the seal, his eyes half closed, looking as if he were falling asleep standing up.

While he hesitates, a few gulls dip to see if they can snatch a quick meal. Mildly annoyed, he swings his forepaw at the birds, not even coming close to their intended flight path.

After feeding on the carcass, the great bear leaves the remaining flesh to the squalling gulls. With measured steps, he begins the gradual climb back to his shelter. Taking the incline in short stages, he paces the hundred-odd yards, bits at a time. When he stops, he slowly swings his head around, watching the hoard of gulls fighting over the seal. Finally reaching his shallow bed, shadowed beneath the cliff, he drops down and falls asleep.

Natural shelters give the polar bear immediate cover from the elements. Dried-up stream beds beneath protective river ice, snow bridges, caves, ridges of ice on icebergs and pack ice—all these are shelters that need little modification before they can be occupied by polar bears. Occasionally the bear will scratch aside a few inches of sand to shape the contour of the ground to his body.

During blizzards in the Arctic regions many Eskimo stories tell of polar bears seeking shelter, stumbling into caves occupied by men. Some men have even walked into caves to find bears already occupying the chamber. Neither men nor bears are usually willing to share their shelter.

Gerrit de Veer wrote:

. . . wee saw a white beare that swamme towardes our shippe; whereupon we left off our worke, and entering into the boate with John Cornelisons men, rowed after her, and crossing her in the way, drove her from the land; where-with shee swamme further into the sea, and wee followed her; and for that our boate could not make way after her, we manned out our small boate also, the better to follow her: but she swamme a mile into the sea; yet wee followed her with the post part of all our men of both ships in three boates, and stroke often times at her, cutting and heawing her, so that all our armes were most broken in peeces. During our fight with her, shee stroke her clawes so hard in our boate, that the signes thereof were seene in it; but as hap was, it was in the forehead of our boate: for if it had been in the middle thereof, she had over-throwne it, they have such force in their clawes. At last, after we had fought long with her, and made her wearie with our three boates that kept about her, we overcame her and killed her: which done, we brought her into our shippe and fleaed her, her skinne being thirteen foote long.

Traveling by different means and routes, the delegates to the First International Scientific Meeting on the Polar Bear converged on Fairbanks, Alaska. For this one week in 1965 the delegates, representing Canada, Denmark, Norway, the U.S.S.R., and the United States, discussed and made recommendations on the conservation of the polar bear.

Realizing that the polar bear is an international resource that must be conserved, the following recommendations were agreed upon by the participants: (1) The circumpolar countries harboring polar bears should begin immediate study on the animal's life history; (2) any information that is learned about the polar bear must be communicated immediately; (3) polar bear harvests must be conservative; (4) if hunting is allowed, females and cubs must be protected.

Concerned by the lack of substantial knowledge, a select few of the conference's delegates left Fairbanks determined to study this polar animal.

Five years later, November 1970, the Second International Conference on Bear Research and Management was held at the University of Calgary, Alberta, Canada. The invited Ursidae researchers presented their papers outlining the results of their recent investigations and innovative techniques.

A small sign outside the lecture hall identified the assembly: "Panel 3: Polar Bear Studies, Dr. Thor Larsen, Chairman." Inside, Dr. Larsen, from Norway's University of Oslo–Institute of Marine Biology, pounded his gavel. He then introduced the first of a group of distinguished polar bear scholars to deliver their papers.

James W. Brooks, a researcher from the United States Bureau of Sport Fisheries and Wildlife Division of Wildlife Research, discussed his attempts and the feasibility of using infrared scanners in airplanes to detect the presence of polar bears on the ice pack. Plagued with numerous problems and difficulties, Dr. Brooks stated: ". . . the initial testing indicated that this method is probably superior to any other and could have applications in line transect sampling systems aimed at yielding estimates of bear numbers over fairly large regions."

During one session the Canadian research team of Charles Jonkel, George Kolenosky, Richard Robertson, and Richard Russell presented the results of their studies of the denning habits of the polar bear population for James Bay and southern Hudson Bay. Comparing their measurements and observations to those in other studies, they have discovered data that point to behavioral differences between the bears in this southern portion of the polar bear's range and the members of the same species in the north. This information will be valuable for future use in defining separate polar bear populations in the Canadian Arctic.

Momentarily relinquishing his role as chairman, Dr. Larsen presented his paper on Norway's management efforts and related research on the polar bear. He cited the existing and new laws regulating polar bear harvest quotas and described what Norway has done to protect the bear. Finally, he suggested projects for the future and new cooperation between his country and the Soviet Union so that their research efforts could be coordinated.

Jack Lentfer, of Alaska's Department of Fish and Game in Barrow, related his observations and studies made off the western and northern coast of Alaska. Having studied the polar bear's relationship to sea ice, Mr. Lentfer discussed the various factors that cause bears to be attracted to certain ice conditions or land areas during the different seasons of the year.

Of special interest were Mr. Lentfer's comments on the effect of human activity in the Arctic regions on the polar bear:

> Consideration should be given to limiting oil-extracting activities in known polar bear denning areas throughout the polar basin. Human activity, including the use of large vehicles and explosive seismic charges, could keep bears away from denning areas. The effects of such activities when bears are in dens or emerging are unknown. Seismic exploration and drilling activities on fast ice could also affect seals, especially ringed seals when they are denning and pupping in the spring.

A conference on polar bears or winter ecology would be incomplete without the energetic Dr. S. M. Uspenski, professor at Moscow State University in the U.S.S.R. He and his research associate, A. A. Kistshinski, presented their first paper describing the techniques they used to immobilize and tag female polar bears. Working on Wrangel Island, a core denning area, they immobilized and marked female bears and their cubs while inside the maternity den. This method enabled them to ease the marking procedure.

With these same immobilizing techniques described in their first paper, they gathered much of the information for their second paper, "New Data on the Winter Ecology of the Polar Bear on Wrangel Island." Traveling by dog team, tractor, tracked vehicle, as well as on foot, they covered more than eight hundred miles during the height of the Arctic winter to gather information, visiting numerous maternity dens. Assessing some of the problems, Dr. Uspenski stated: "[The] biology of the polar bear in winter, when parturition takes place, had been poorly studied up to recently. Only of late have these researches made progress and papers have appeared dealing with winter ecology of the species in different Arctic regions. Many aspects of the problem are still far from clear."

Leaving this conference, the participants no doubt felt more encouraged than they had five years earlier when they left the First International Meeting on the polar bear. Great progress has been made, but the future cannot be taken for granted. Cooperation with other Ursidae specialists must continue, international exchange should increase, new techniques and equipment have to be developed, and research must be expanded. The search for knowledge must continue.

A mother polar bear and her cub wander along Shugliak's eastern coast, searching for carrion and any other available food. For the two bears, particularly the mother, it has been a difficult summer. The she-bear looks emaciated and tired. They have had little success hunting for seals, and the male cub has had to depend heavily on his mother's supply of milk for the greater portion of the summer. Unsuccessful in today's search for food, the two find a protected hollow and dig a small pit to sleep in. For one day the mother bear does not leave her bed. Suffering from tuberculosis, a disease not uncommon among polar bears, she has great difficulty breathing.

That night the mother bear dies. The cub, upon waking, senses something wrong, but continues to scratch in the snow, looking for food. Guarding his mother, he stays at her side for two days. While searching for food, the cub spots a pack of wolves prowling along the coast. As he scampers back to his mother's side, the wolves sight the cub and follow him. Two of the three wolves go after the motionless bear. The third wolf chases the cub from his mother's side. Without his mother's protection, the cub is lucky the wolves ignore him in favor of his mother.

The cub continues on his own. The first two weeks are difficult, but with a tenacious hold on life he continues. Scavenging and using the few skills taught to him by his mother, he is able to survive.

OCTOBER
OOKIAK—The Days When
the Islands in the Bay
Freeze Shut

With the progression of autumn days, the appearance of the aurora borealis becomes more frequent, growing stronger and brighter each night. Pale yellows, reds, purples, lacy pinks bordered with green flare across the sky. Often the lights slowly transverse the sky, easing in and across like banks of fog. Others roll, billow, and even seem to explode like storm clouds. Whether they quiver or flare, the mysterious lights seem only to emphasize the already eerie desolation.

Growing from the coves and bays, the ice sheet swallows the islets, progressing farther and farther each cold day. Heavy snow falls for five straight days. The tundra is now covered with a thick layer of snow.

Wolves can be heard howling in the distance, as if lamenting the return of winter's cold and snow. Almost all the snow buntings have flown south. With the ice sheet moving out and covering the beached seaweed, the purple sandpipers have left Shugliak. The summer birds, migrating south, are replaced by the arrival of great flocks of ptarmigan. Each ptarmigan is now covered with white winter plumage, ready for the long, winter months ahead.

The mate Little Cub's father chose last April has followed almost the same pattern of existence as Little Cub's family. Back on Shugliak Island once again, she prepares to face the cold, lonely winter. She is getting ready to give birth to a litter of cubs.

Just like their relative the badger, pregnant female polar bears display delayed implantation. Approximately eight to ten weeks before parturition, but months after fertilization occurs, the waiting blastocyst, a microscopic embryo, implants itself in the uterus wall. If the pregnant female is in satisfactory condition, the timed internal changes will alert her to begin prospecting for a den. Six weeks before they give birth, the gravid females become lethargic and irritable, but fortunately they are in their dens.

How do we know implantation is delayed? From scientifically oriented hunters' records, as well as from Eskimo accounts, we learn that very few females carrying detectable embryos have ever been killed before winter denning occurs. The pregnancy term of the female polar bear and that of a woman are almost the same length of time, but the important factors to consider are the size and weight. The polar bear cub at birth is almost one-seventh the size and weight of the human baby. Delayed implantation, induced by hormones, is responsible.

Little Cub, his mother, and his sister awake to find themselves covered by yesterday's snowstorm. Protected from the howling wind, the fluffy snow has piled deep. With the polar night lasting longer and longer each day, Little Cub's mother knows they must soon find a den. Still drowsy, the three begin to follow the seashore north.

Having traveled many miles from Seahorse Point, they

are now just a few miles below Cape Comfort. Watching carefully, the great she-bear searches for a stream bed to follow inland. When she sees familiar cliffs standing several hundred feet above the ocean, she knows her search will end soon. Between the cliffs an already frozen-over stream leading inland guides the bears closer to their destination. They spend all day climbing the rocky stream bed. Finally they reach a series of gullies, well concealed by deep drifts of snow piled by the winds. Here Little Cub's family will begin prospecting for a site to dig their den.

In 1634 Van der Brugge, overwintering with his men on the northwestern coast of West Spitsbergen, related some of the findings of his explorations during the month of February: "We then walked about the country, and saw in high, steep places on the mountains great caves, where the bears had made their camps, two of our comrades getting up to them after much trouble."

Gerrit de Veer, stranded along with Barents on the coast of northeastern Novaya Zemlya during the winter of 1597, describes the confrontation his party had with a polar bear and the subsequent exploration of her den. He is probably the first man to write a description of a polar bear's den:

> . . . there came a great beare towards us, against whom we began to make defence, but she perceaving that, made away from us, and we went to the place from whence she came to see her den, where we found a great hole made in the ice, about a mans length in depth, the entry thereof being very narrow, and within wide; there we thrust in our pikes to feele if there was anything within it, but perceaving it was emptie, one of our men crept into it, but not too farre, for it was fearefull to behold.

The primary core polar bear denning areas are spread around the northern portion of our hemisphere; northeastern and western Greenland, eastern Svalbard, Franz Josef Land, Wrangel Island, southern Banks Island, Simpson Peninsula, eastern Baffin Island, and eastern Southampton Island. Of secondary importance are the areas on the southern Hudson Bay coast; Novaya Zemlya, Severnaya Zemlya, Taimyr Peninsula, New Siberian Islands, Bear Islands, and Chukchi Peninsula. Dens can also be found peppered inconspicuously throughout many other Arctic areas.

What do these locations have in common that is attractive to polar bears? Offshore of these localities are ice fields that support large populations of seals, the polar bear's favorite food. Fjords, river valleys, and mountains are also present to collect deep deposits of snow. With both of these prerequisites available, the polar bear returns to these areas year after year.

Little Cub, his mother, and his sister spend much time prospecting for the site of their winter den. Some drifts they have examined have been well protected, lasting over the summer months. These drifts are too icy, almost impossible to dig through. Other drifts consist of snow that is too fluffy, affording little protection from wind and snow. Finally the she-bear finds a drift that suits her. Scratching with her forepaw, she digs into the drift and begins the entry hole. The farther she digs into the deposit, the greater the pile of displaced snow behind her.

Polar bear dens are classified as maternity dens, natural shelters, or temporary dens. Maternity dens are excavated by a solitary pregnant female. Usually consisting of one or more rooms, they are inhabited as long as six months. In autumn pregnant females seem to concentrate in core areas, mainly because of pack ice movement that directs them to these certain areas.

Natural shelters may be characterized as any previously existing structures that provide protection against adverse weather elements. With little or no modification, they may be occupied for a few hours or for many days.

Temporary dens are excavated by adult males, non-pregnant females, and immature bears. Such dens are occupied from one day to as long as four months. Nonpregnant females and older males will generally stay inside for the duration of the extremely harsh weather. Usually this type of den has one large room with a number of small, shallow pockets scraped into the snow.

Once either the maternity or temporary den has been excavated, it is difficult to detect its presence. If one is observant, it is possible to spot the polar bear's tracks leading to the entry hole, but a snowstorm or blowing, drifting snow can easily conceal the tracks. Wisps of steam, small accumulations of snow, and a rim of black spots around the ventilation hole may mark the den. With the den so well camouflaged, trained husky bear dogs are often the only sure way of finding dens.

After hours of arduous work the she-bear completes her den. Tired after their long journey inland, searching for the site, and digging the den, they enter it for the first time to rest.

Beginning his autumn search for seals, Little Cub's father has returned to the ice floes off Shugliak Island. Once again the he-bear is in the midst of the noisy ice pack. Stefansson vividly describes the sounds of the pack:

> When the ice is being piled against a polar coast there is a high-pitched screeching as one cake slides over the other, like the thousand-times magnified creaking of a rusty hinge. There is the crashing when cakes as big as a church wall, after being tilted on edge, finally pass beyond their equilibrium and topple down upon the ice; and when extensive floes, perhaps six or more feet in thickness, gradually bend under the resistless pressure of the pack until they buckle up and snap, there is a groaning as of super giants in torment and a booming which at a distance of a mile or two sounds like a cannonade.

The polar bear's sense of hearing is of little value while he moves across the pack ice. It is almost impossible to detect specific noises in the howling wind and grinding ice. Because of the excessive noise in his environment, the polar bear probably ignores most of the sounds he hears. In fact, some polar bears do not react to the sound of a rifle shot.

With the return of the ice from the northeast, sealing is good again. Concerned over the onset of winter weather, the he-bear begins his search for seals to fatten his layers of blubber.

Waking from her sleep, Little Cub's mother knows that they must return to the ocean to fatten themselves for the coming winter. Having excavated their winter den, the three begin their return trek to the ocean.

It is difficult to attribute the onset of denning to any one particular stimulus. Fat reserves, abundance of food, and climatic conditions all are factors in determining the timing of denning. If Little Cub's family had sufficient layers of fat and the weather became harsh, the three would return to their previously excavated den. Since the weather is now good and seals are available, they will delay the date of denning as long as possible. A definite behavioral change is occurring with almost all of the polar bears on Shugliak Island. The listlessness that accompanied late summer and early autumn has been replaced by a more energetic life style. Instead of the slow, methodical pace, Little Cub and his family move toward the ocean with renewed vigor and anticipation of the return to seal hunting.

Now that ice on the bays and coves is thickening and becoming harder, seals living there must begin concentrating in one area to keep their breathing holes open over the long winter. In some areas during October great numbers of seals can be seen on the ice beside their hole.

There are a number of different methods Little Cub's mother can use to capture a seal at his breathing hole. With the ice only four inches thick, the she-bear can use her paw to break holes and wait for a seal to breathe. Some polar hunters even claim polar bears pack as many breathing holes as they can find in one area and then hunt at the only one they have left open. No matter where or how a breathing hole is found, Little Cub, his mother, and his sister must wait at one hole for long periods of time before a seal visits it. Eskimos can attest to the long waits while they have been hunting for seals.

Little Cub's mother must first scrape away the top layers of ice and snow from the breathing hole, opening the hole wide enough to insert her claw. Sitting back, the she-bear begins her wait. Little Cub and his sister, tired from their return trek to the ice, lie down near a small ridge of ice and rest.

Watching carefully, the she-bear does not have to wait long before she is rewarded. A seal breaks the surface at the breathing hole. Immediately striking, the she-bear, using her claw, drags the seal out of the hole and flips it on the ice in one flowing motion. Quickly joining their mother, the two cubs begin the long-awaited blubber feast.

Cirrus, the polar bear cub captured in Greenland, has been living in his bear grotto since last May. When he first arrived, the zoo's veterinarian supervised the cub's release into his forty-by-fifty-foot home. Still dizzy from his bumpy ride in the back of the zoo's truck, he spent the first day in the zoo trying to clear his head.

Once he had investigated his grotto, he found he was trapped in the small area, unable to escape. With tall walls on three sides, it is impossible for Cirrus to climb out. The fourth side, though open, has a moat preventing escape. Since many animals are capable of leaping great distances, the front portion of the grotto is sloped downward, preventing bounds of any distance. In the back of the grotto a small pool of water is filled daily so the bear can cool off in the humid air. Behind the pool is a small den for sleeping away from the hot sun and curious crowds. The small quarters are not exactly the same as the fjords and ice floes of Greenland.

Until a few weeks ago Cirrus was alone. With a great deal of apprehension the zoo's veterinarian transferred the other polar bear to Cirrus's grotto. The two bears immediately began sniffing each other. To the relief of the zoo's staff, the bears turned around and, except for occasional brief play sessions, ignored each other.

The other polar bear, a female, was recently given to the zoo by a civic group in Abilene, Texas. Their veterinarian, deciding that the nineteen-year-old bear could no longer stand the hot Texas weather, appealed to the zoo's administration to find a new, cooler environment. The town's civic group was able to find the older bear a new home in the upper Midwest, where weather is usually more suitable for polar bears.

For the two bears in the grotto, life is monotonous. Cirrus spends most of his day pacing back and forth across the grotto. He walks forty feet one way, turns, and walks back forty feet to the other side. Accustomed to wandering in open spaces, the bear has energy to spare and cannot lie still. Stopping every so often, Cirrus sniffs to detect what is in the near vicinity. The polar bear grotto is directly downwind from the seal's pool; no doubt the musky odor reminds him of his hunting experiences and the fishy-tasting blubber.

The monotony of the day is broken only by their zookeeper bringing them their food. As they are carnivorous animals, the zoo provides them with a daily ration of horse meat, not quite the same as the craved seal blubber. With some frequency their diet is supplemented with fruit and stale bread.

Adult polar bears have very few health problems while in captivity. The greatest threat they have is from their observers, some only done as acts of friendship, others maliciously. Assorted candies, peanuts, popcorn, and a variety of leftovers from picnic lunches are thrown to the bears. The zoo's vet could attest to the damage done to the bears' teeth and general health by these sweet treats. He would be happy to show any offender the box holding polar bears' decayed teeth that he has had to extract over the years. The malicious acts do not deserve our attention. Persons harming animals, no matter how large or small, belong in a class apart.

There are few zoos in the world with proper facilities and equipment to raise wild animals from infancy to adulthood. Pregnant females and mothers seem to lose their maternal instinct once caged in a zoo. Most animals will mate while captive, but they refuse to care for their offspring. Few infants can be taken from their mothers before they are injured or exposed to adverse weather conditions. The polar bear is no exception to this rule. Consequently, unless there are rather sophisticated facilities available, the newborn cubs are doomed.

Only a few of the world's zoos have taken the responsibility to breed their captive stock in an effort to perpetuate the various wild species. The polar bear cubs, living outside of their almost bacteria-free Arctic environment, are now more susceptible to infections. Special facilities similiar to hospital nurseries are required—incubators, sterilization equipment, special synthetic polar bear milk formulas, and something for which there is no substitute—tender, loving care.

Famous throughout the world for its success in raising polar bears is the Washington Park Zoological Garden in Milwaukee, Wisconsin. The prolific dam, Sultana, first became cyclic in 1919. During the spring she mated with the zoo's dominant male, Silver King. On December 2, 1919, she gave birth to the first polar bear cub that was ever successfully reared in captivity. From 1919 until 1935 Sultana produced a total of twelve cubs—eleven of which were successfully raised. These twelve cubs were born in alternate years in litters of one or two.

Records kept of polar bear longevity while in captivity also give us a general idea of their life span while living in the wild. Sultana from Washington Park Zoological Garden was thirty-four years of age when she died. The oldest male living in captivity was forty-one years of age when he died at the Zoological Garden of Chester, England.

In Washington, D.C., at the Zoological Park, Dr. William Mann has crossed the Kodiak brown bear, found in Alaska, and the polar bear. The resulting hybrids have never lived long, due to parental neglect. In January 1950, with the birth of another litter, the mother nursed the litter for one week and then lost interest. The zookeepers, seeing the neglected cub, were able to remove the small bear, immediately warming him in a blanket and feeding him milk with an eyedropper. His color was described as a tawny yellow, similar to the color of a palomino horse. During the spring Little Gene, as he was christened, became the number-one star attraction of the zoo.

Dr. R. C. Cook, a geneticist studying Little Gene, discusses the case:

> The significance of the interfertility of the two Arctic zone species is hard to appraise since so little has been done in Ursine genetics. It is hoped that Little Gene is only a harbinger of a larger crop of siblings and cousins in the years to come. Will they show, as might be expected in the F_2 [next] generation of such a cross, brown, white, and khaki coloration? Will some of them take to the sea and will others cleave to the land? We can hardly bear to wait for time to give us the answer.

There has long been a conflict over the worth and humaneness of displaying animals in zoos. It is not a difficult task to point out the shortcomings of most of these institutions. Except for a select few, the majority of the world's zoos are guilty of poor and inadequate conditions. Confining animals in cages and grottos, totally different from their normal environment, is cruel. Enclosed within their artificial surroundings, they are also the target of inevitable, malicious pranks.

On the other hand, there are those who argue that zoos

are valuable and justify the confinement of the world's diminishing and rare species of animals. Observing the zoos' visitors as they view the exhibits provides much insight into its importance. Watching the expression of excitement and delight on the faces of children as their mothers show them the animals is a strong plus on the pro side. Schoolchildren accompanied by their teachers can learn much through the teachers' careful questioning, using the child's previously learned knowledge.

In many respects the zoos are not being used to the best of their capabilities. Very little if any scientific study is carried out. Many aspects of the animals' behavior and physiology are different from what they are in normal circumstances, yet data gathered in the zoos can serve as a basis of comparison in field studies. With man's continued encroachment on animals' territory, zoos can serve as breeding reservoirs to insure the perpetuation of endangered species.

Most zoo administrators would have to agree that there should be strict legislation controlling the living conditions and safety standards in zoos. These laws would no doubt ease the animals' discomfort while being displayed and improve the zoos' atmosphere.

Little Cub's father, like most other Shugliak polar bears, is returning to the sea to hunt for seals. He walks out on an ice-covered bay and begins the search for seal breathing holes. Hearing unusual gasps and water splashing nearby, he curiously heads in the direction of the noise. With the sudden drop in temperatures in the past few days, the water has been freezing fast. Trapped in a frozen current hole, the swimming unicorn of the Arctic, a narwhal, swims back and forth in his ice prison, fighting to keep his head above the surface for a breath of air. When the ice is from six to eight inches thick, it is impossible for the narwhal to break through back into open spaces. Seeing the trapped narwhal, the he-bear leaps down on the animal, slaying it with his massive paw. He pulls the narwhal to the edge of the ice, hauls it out of the current hole, and feasts on the marine mammal. Eskimos have reported seeing as many as fifteen to twenty-five young narwhals imprisoned in frozen current holes and pulled out one after another by a polar bear.

NOVEMBER
KHIANGULIUT—
The Season of Ice
Around the Ocean Shore

From the north, savage winds numb Shugliak Island. After a two-day blizzard deep gray clouds, bled of their fury, back off, yielding to the clear, cold sky. An ice band is clasped around the island. High tide fills the shore's void basins, leaving diamond crystals. Steaming and smoking, the water glows above the ice clusters. The noonday sun drops lower and lower each passing day. Fading daylight leaves Shugliak Island exposed to the beginning of winter's bitter cold.

For the past month Little Cub, his mother, and his sister have been hunting on the band of ice around and on the ice floes floating by Shugliak Island. Having had good luck capturing seals and also finding a bloated walrus carcass, the three have been able to build their fat reserves. With the onset of bitter cold and freezing wind, Little Cub's mother decides it is time to return to their den.

Little Cub and his sister have grown rapidly during the spring, summer, and autumn. Little Cub now measures four feet in length and weighs more than 140 pounds. Overwintering without seal blubber to eat, the two cubs' growth will cease while they sleep in the den.

It will be some time before Little Cub and his sister are fully grown. Maturing more rapidly than males, female cubs are full-grown at the age of four years. Smaller than males, the female cub will reach six feet in length and weigh 700 pounds at maturity. Little Cub, like most other male polar bears, will not reach maximum growth until the age of six. Usually reaching nine feet in length and weighing close to 1000 pounds, the male of the species is a formidable creature, walking tall among the multifarious members of the animal kingdom.

The mate Little Cub's father chose last April sleeps on in her den. Within her womb the implanted, microscopic blastocyst, now being nourished, grows. Taking shape, the ball of cells expands—ridges, bulges, pockets, swellings, and ripples are molded into the minute embryo. Pregnancy has brought on the deep, lethargic sleep with which the she-bear conserves her energy for the tiny bear. It will not be a long wait until, for the first time, the she-bear will become a mother.

Two scholars, Dr. C. R. Harington of Canada and Dr. S. M. Uspenski of the Soviet Union, have been world leaders in the scientific study of the denning habits of the polar bear. Struggling against severe weather conditions, both of these dedicated scientists have added considerable knowledge on the life of the polar bear. Describing some of the difficulties, Dr. Harington states: "The inaccessibility of the denning range and the inconspicuousness of the dens, together with the rigorous weather conditions that prevail during the denning period, hinder study."

He has completed many of his studies on Little Cub's home island, and his results tell us much about the winter denning habit.

For many of the polar bears on Shugliak Island, the

search for a denning site begins in October. By the middle of December most of the bears will be in their dens—except, of course, the males still hunting on the ice floes, where they will spend most of the winter. Pregnant females, single adult females, females with cubs, and old adult males will remain in their dens until late March or early April. Excluding pregnant females, eventually joined by their cubs, and first-year bears living with their mothers, the remaining polar bears will den by themselves for the winter.

The duration of denning varies among the different members of the species and depends on environmental factors. A pregnant female, after delivering her cubs, will spend the longest time in the den. Protecting her newborn cubs, she will remain in the maternity den for as long as 170 days. Non-pregnant females, unencumbered by cubs, will stay in the den as long as 125 days. Families, similar to Little Cub's, will last approximately 105 days. Immature adults and old males will remain in their den only 60 days.

When it is time for denning, polar bears have always retreated to their stable, primeval home—the land. As ecologists complete their tagging studies, more evidence is found indicating that female polar bears return again and again to their ancestral core denning areas. Some scientists have even suggested that the same females return to the same vicinity of their denning site year after year.

The polar bear, depending on the ocean for food, does not trek extreme distances to find a denning site. Walking five to ten miles inland, the bears remain close to the shore. Thirty miles inland is the farthest most bears travel to find a den.

In search of deep snowdrifts, polar bears often locate their dens on slopes facing south. On these slopes, especially in Canada, the prevailing winds from the north build drifts perfectly suited to the needs of the polar bear. These drifts have insulation properties that will protect the bears from the extremely low temperatures. Inside the drift the piercing wind chill is at a minimal level. In the spring southern-facing slopes are the warmest areas for cubs to run, play, and bask in the sun.

In years of small amounts of precipitation, autumn snows leave few drifts capable of protecting polar bears. Denning in some areas is delayed until sufficient snow falls. In such years bears suffer greatly from exposure to the cold and wind.

The process of den excavation and preparation begins with the polar bear choosing a snowbank with acceptable density and depth. Using the forepaws and beginning with the entrance way, the bear will dig out the drift. The excavation is a work of precision. The walls are carefully carved and packed. Snow is swept out and deposited outside the entrance way. During the winter both body heat and physical pressure enlarge the den. The inside of the den is marked with paw scratches on the walls, prints from the bear's muzzle on the floor, and indentations on the ceiling, where his back was pressed.

In a core denning area two dens have been found to be as close as fifty feet apart. The highest density within one region has had as many as nine dens in a twenty-eight-square-mile area. As the techniques of finding dens and tracking polar bears becomes more proficient, the concentration may be found to be even greater.

Dr. Harington has described and sketched many of the maternity dens he found on Southampton Island. Polar bear dens have often been described as the prototype of the Eskimo's igloo. Each den is unique, due to the size and location of the drift, and, most important, the design of the individual bear. The entrance ways are usually at least three and a half feet long and two and a half feet wide. The height of the entrance way and the rest of the den ranges from over one and a half feet to almost four feet. The passageway slopes upward, preventing the escape of the warm air from the interior. Found between the entrance way and inner rooms are small ridges or sills— structures that also conserve the den's heat. Some rooms are rectangular, with dimensions of four feet by thirteen feet. Many rooms are circular in shape—six feet by seven feet. Along the walls are small alcoves, hollowed out by the cubs' play or gnawed out during the long winter months by thirsty adults.

The den is completely surrounded by snow and may lie as deep as ten feet below the surface of the snow, depending on the amount of drifting snow deposited over the winter months. The ventilation hole, a tube three inches in diameter, provides the bears with air—a necessity in their sealed den. This hole is regulated constantly throughout the winter by the bear to control den temperatures.

For the past few months Little Cub's father has been hunting on the drifting ice floes off Shugliak Island. With November's gale from the northeast, he has been blown back to the northern coast of the island. Walking on the land-fast ice, the great he-bear finds a musk-marked seal breathing hole.

Having had little to eat in the past three days, he begins his vigil, waiting for the seal to breathe. First, he scrapes away the upper layer of snow and ice from the hole. Then the air hole is enlarged to allow him to thrust his forepaw in.

The great he-bear now begins his long wait. Crouching three feet from the seal's breathing hole, he lays his head on his extended paws. In this posture, which he can hold for a long period of time, he can strike the seal immediately, once it breaks the surface. Polar explorers and hunters have found worn-down beds in the ice and snow, made by polar bears waiting for seals to breathe.

During the various seasons of the year there are five different species of seals in the vicinity of Shugliak Island. Found most frequently are the bearded, ringed, and hooded seals—occasionally a harbor and harp seal will be sighted. During the colder seasons when ice covers much of the open water, seals are forced to use aglos, or breathing holes. The ice around the aglos can be as thick as from three to seven feet, with exceptional instances of ice as thick as ten feet deep. These aglos are shaped like long bells. Ten to twelve breathing holes are used during a winter, and the seal must take care in gnawing away the ice to keep his aglos from freezing over. Biologists believe the seal finds his breathing hole by marking it with a musky scent. Older seals are known for their enduring, strong odor that permeates the breathing hole and the air around it.

Hours pass slowly; still no seal. The cold wind blows and chills the bear. Without warning the water is broken and the seal blows loudly. The he-bear strikes instantly, grabbing the seal, and pulls him out of his hole. Rewarded for his patience, the he-bear feasts on the seal.

The polar bear is not the only creature seeking the elusive seal. Near Cape Low on the southern coast of Shugliak Island, an Eskimo awakes from his sleep. He pulls on his pants made from the pelt of a caribou and begins dressing in his inner clothing. Long, loose-fitting socks are pulled up and packed with dry grasses. Over the socks slipper-like low boots are worn. Since the weather is bitterly cold and windy, high boots, covered with fur on the outside, are drawn over the low ones. The warm caribou pants are loosely tucked into the high boots.

A hooded tunic, made of soft fur with the fur facing the inside, collects warm air from the body. Fitting snugly, made of nonporous pelts with tightly sewed seams, the tunic conserves much of the body heat. The outer tunic is added to the outfit. Wolf's fur, one of nature's few that does not collect ice from the breath's moisture, is sewed around the hood for extra warmth. Mittens that extend to the elbows are loosely fitted over the hands. Completely dressed, the Eskimo wears an outfit that weighs only ten pounds—Americans and Europeans facing the same weather in their carefully manufactured clothes would add thirty pounds to their frame before they would feel as warm.

Carrying his rifle and harpoon, the Eskimo leaves the encampment and walks on the half-mile-wide band of ice that skirts the island. Finally he locates a mound of ice that marks a seal's breathing hole. He stands still over the hole and waits for the seal to breathe. A gale from the northeast blasts the island. With so little fresh meat in his village there is no choice but to hunt in the cold. One—two—three hours without a seal, only the vicious, chilling wind.

Suddenly a great mass of ice breaks free and he begins to drift, sailing fast with the wind. Only a crack at first, it quickly widens into a broad, expansive channel—floating away from the island.

At the camp an Eskimo woman sees the great mass of ice breaking free and watches it move away slowly. Finally she realizes the hunter is drifting away. Screaming into the wind, she whips the village into action. The frightened Eskimos, pouring out of every door, race to help. One man runs as best he can across the rough ice to his canoe and slides into the water. He paddles through the channel's choppy waves toward the drifting ice.

As he creeps across the ice, the terrified seal hunter can no longer see the island through the storm. After an eternity the hunter sees the canoe bouncing across the waves. Now, sailing with the wind, the canoe quickly catches the drifting mass of ice. With great difficulty the paddler sidles up to the ice to rescue the hunter. With every second they are pushed farther and farther from the island.

At the edge of the ice Eskimos from the camp shield their eyes from the wind, struggling to see the men. They cannot see far in the blowing snow. Gradually they return to the camp. Their usual smiles and laughter are gone; their eyes are sad, their lips compressed. The sun drops and evening hushes the village. Occasionally an Eskimo slips outside his door and scrutinizes the horizon, begging for their return. Tonight not a man or woman sleeps without dreaming of the two men in the black, frigid darkness—will they be heard from again?

Battling the gale, the two men can hardly move. For

hour after hour they have pulled with their paddles. If they stop, they know, the end will be soon.

In the distance a small light flickers through the wind, guiding the men to their village. New strength flows through their arms, and they exert themselves with every ounce of muscle left. At last the bow of their boat grates into the ice around Shugliak and the two crawl onto the stationary land-held ice. They leave the canoe on the ice and walk the half mile to the camp.

A screech from behind a window wakes the camp, and the villagers run to their exhausted comrades. The two men will long be the source of heroic storytelling. Neither of them needs to be reminded of the seal hunt that left them on the precarious edge of life and death for hours of painful struggling.

Words written on conservation of the polar bear will never quite match Vagn Flyger's in his commentary, "The Polar Bear: A Matter for International Concern":

> Although it is the nations bordering the polar seas that demonstrate the greatest interest in the polar bear, he actually belongs to everyone. Surely the peoples of the world would want to assure this great animal a permanent place on the globe, not because he is something for hunters to shoot, but because he is a symbol of the Arctic and a worthy companion of mankind. . . . The polar bear is part of the world's heritage and has an aesthetic value probably far in excess of his economic value to hunters. Nevertheless, both values must be considered if and when an international regulating body is formed to set management policy and to coordinate research on the polar bear. The important thing now is to set the wheels in motion for the formation of the international commission. . . . The polar bear definitely merits international concern and action.

Little Cub, his mother, and his sister, landing on Shugliak Island, begin their trek, returning to their excavated den. Little Cub's mother has three inches of blubber on her back, buttocks, and thighs. The two cubs, though not so well equipped, have sufficient fat to see them through the winter.

The three crawl up the rocky stream bed once again and head for their refuge from the bitter cold and chilling wind. When they finally reach the den, the great she-bear must dig out some of the snow that has almost blocked the passageway. Once their way has been cleared, the three crawl through the low passage. The mother bear packs the entrance and seals the three into the den, away from nature's violent weather. After adjusting the ventilation hole, the she-bear joins her cubs, curled up, ready to begin their deep winter sleep.

In the dens nearby the cries of pain are quickly replaced by whimpers of newborn cubs. The new cubbing season begins.

The year of the polar bear has ended. These great creatures warm this frigid world—challenged by many, conquered by few. Little Cub will grow and live in this desolate cold. With time's passing, he will slowly become "Nanook—the great white bear of the North." Let us insure his survival.

REFERENCE NOTES

MONTH
HEADINGS
TAKEN FROM:

G. M. Sutton *Eskimo Year, A Naturalist's Adventures in the Far North*. New York: The Macmillan Company, 1934. Thule Expedition (5th) 1921–1924. Report #3. Gyldendalske Boghandel, Nordisk Forlag, Copenhagen, 1941.

PAGE AND
LINE

4:26–31
Albert Hastings Markham *The Voyages and Works of John Davis*. London: The Hakluyt Society, 1880, page 10.

5:29–33
6:1–8
Vilhjalmur Stefansson *The Friendly Arctic*. New York: The Macmillan Company, 1943, pages 289–290.

7:4–11
John Muir *The Cruise of the Corwin—Journal of the Arctic Expedition of 1881 in Search of De Long and the Jeannette*. Boston: Houghton-Mifflin Company, 1917, pages 156 and 177.

7:22–33
Vilhjalmur Stefansson *Hunters of the Great North*. New York: Harcourt, Brace and Company, 1922, page 272.

12:11
The words "carnivorean lethargy" are credited to: R. J. Hock "Seasonal Variations in Physiologic Functions of Arctic Ground Squirrels and Black Bears." *Bulletin Museum Comparative Zoology Harvard* 124 (1960), page 155.

21:18–23
J. W. Tyrrel *Across the Sub-Arctic of Canada*. Toronto: William Buggs, 1897.

24:1–13
G. M. Sutton *Eskimo Year, A Naturalist's Adventures in the Far North*. New York: The Macmillan Company, 1934, pages 56–57.

25:5–27
Vagn Flyger "The Polar Bear: A Matter for International Concern." *Arctic* 20(3) (1967), page 148.

26:32–33
Vagn Flyger "The Polar Bear: A Matter for International Concern." *Arctic* 20(3) (1967), pages 149–150.

33:8–11
Robert Peary *Northward Over the Great Ice*. New York: Frederick Stokes Company, 1898, page 374.

33:31–32 34:1–3	Vilhjalmur Stefansson *The Friendly Arctic*. New York: The Macmillan Company, 1943, page 213.
34:7–19	Fridtjof Nansen *Farthest North*. New York: Harper and Brothers Publisher, 1897, pages 338–342.
36:32–33 37:1–34	Vilhjalmur Stefansson *My Life with the Eskimo*. New York: The Macmillan Company, 1924, pages 57–58.
38:1–13	Sydney R. Montague *North to Adventure*. New York: Robert M. McBride and Company, 1939, page 188.
38:22–27	The quote ". . . and drest and eat . . ." is credited to: Sir John Richardson *The Polar Regions*. Edinburgh: Adam and Charles Black, 1861, page 71.
38:29–35 39:1–3	Elisha Kent Kane *Arctic Explorations in the Years 1853, '54, '55*. Philadelphia: Childs and Peterson, 1855, Vol. I, page 382.
51:20–35 52:1–13	Vilhjalmur Stefansson *The Friendly Arctic*. New York: The Macmillan Company, 1943, page 156.
52:16–35	Elisha Kent Kane *Arctic Explorations in the Years 1853, '54, '55*. Philadelphia: Childs and Peterson, 1855, pages 276–278.
53:2–18	Richard Perry *The World of the Polar Bear*. Seattle: University of Washington Press, 1966, page 144.
55, 56, 57, 58:1–14	Vagn Flyger and Marjorie R. Townsend "The Migration of Polar Bears." *Scientific American* 218(2) (1968), pages 115–116.
66:11–24	Frederick Schwatka *Nimrod in the North or Hunting and Fishing Adventures in the Arctic Regions*. New York: Cassell and Company Limited, 1885, page 33.
73:14–36 74, 75:1–4	Martin Schein and F. M. Hart "A Close Look at Polar Bears." *Animal Kingdom* 65(6) (1962), pages 163–165, 167–168.
77:5–15	Joaquin Miller *True Bear Stories*. Chicago: Rand, McNally and Co., 1900, page 152.
78:321–32 79:1–16	Vilhjalmur Stefansson *The Friendly Arctic*. New York: The Macmillan Company, 1943, pages 305–306.
81:19–35 82:1–6	The quote "[A walrus] rose in a pool . . ." is credited to: Capt. F. W. Beechey *A Voyage of Discovery Towards the North Pole*. London: Richard Bentley, 1843, pages 82–83.

86:1–14 Frank Illingworth *Wild Life Beyond the North*. New York: Charles Scribner's Sons, 1952, pages 102–103.

88:23–34
89:1–3 Gerrit de Veer *The Three Voyages of William Barents to the Arctic Regions*. London: The Hakluyt Society, 1853, page 169.

89:8–36
90:1–7 Captain Koldeway *The German Arctic Expedition of 1869–70*. London: Sampson Low, Marston, Low, and Searle, 1874, pages 395–397.

90:10–30 Ernest Seton *Lives of Game Animals*. New York: Doubleday, Doran and Company, 1929, Vol. II, Part I, page 220.

91:3–10 The quote "He [a native of Upernivik] . . ." is credited to: Captain M'Clintock *The Voyage of the "Fox" in the Arctic Seas. A Narrative of the Discovery of the Fate of Sir John Franklin and His Companions*. Boston: Ticknor and Fields, 1860, pages 93–94.

91:11–17 Richard Perry *The World of the Polar Bear*. Seattle: University of Washington Press, 1966, page 46. (Secondary source.)

91:19–35
92:1–17 Alwin Pederson *Polar Animals*. New York: Taplinger Publishing Co. Inc., pages 103–104.

93:13–31 Jack W. Lentfer "Polar Bear—Sea Ice Relationship." Paper from the Second International Conference on Bear Research and Management. Morges, Switzerland, *International Union for Conservation of Nature and Natural Resources*. (IUCN) (1970), pages 170–171.

94:1–6 C. J. Jonkel "Some Comments on Polar Bear Management." *Biological Conservation* 2(2) (1970), page 117.

99:8–24 Sir Martin Conway *Early Dutch and English Voyages to Spitsbergen in the Seventeenth Century*. London: The Hakluyt Society, 1902, pages 124, 125, and 136.

101:19–33
102, 103:1–6 Gerrit de Veer *The Three Voyages of William Barents to the Arctic Regions*. London: The Hakluyt Society, 1853, pages 63–64.

103:9–22 Frederick Schwatka *Nimrod in the North or Hunting and Fishing Adventures in the Arctic Regions*. New York: Cassell and Company Limited, 1885, page 21.

106:20–27   Gerrit de Veer *The Three Voyages of William Barents to the Arctic Regions.* London: The Hakluyt Society, 1853, pages 109–110.

108:5–25   Gerrit de Veer *The Three Voyages of William Barents to the Arctic Regions.* London: The Hakluyt Society, 1853, pages 78–79.

109:25–28   J. W. Brooks "Infra-red Scanning for Polar Bears." Paper from the Second International Conference on Bear Research and Management. Morges, Switzerland, *International Union for Conservation of Nature and Natural Resources.* (IUCN) (1970), page 171.

110:21–29   J. W. Lentfer "Polar Bear—Sea Ice Relationship." Paper from the Second International Conference on Bear Research and Management. Morges, Switzerland, *International Union for Conservation of Nature and Natural Resources.* (IUCN) (1970), page 170.

111:12–17   S. M. Uspenski and A. A. Kistchinski "New Data on the Winter Ecology of the Polar Bear on Wrangel Island." Paper from the Second International Conference on Bear Research and Management. Morges, Switzerland, *International Union for Conservation of Nature and Natural Resources.* (IUCN) (1970), page 181.

115:14–17   Sir Martin Conway *Early Dutch and English Voyages to Spitsbergen in the Seventeenth Century.* London: The Hakluyt Society, 1902, page 142.

115:18–27   Gerrit de Veer *The Three Voyages of William Barents to the Arctic Regions.* London: The Hakluyt Society, 1853, pages 170–171.

117:23–33   Vilhjalmur Stefansson *The Friendly Arctic.* New York: The Macmillan Company, 1943, pages 19–20.

122:16–24   R. C. Cook "Gene—The Hybrid Bear." *Journal of Heredity* 41(2) (1950), page 34.

126:26–29   C. R. Harrington "Denning Habits of the Polar Bear (Ursus maritimus Phipps)." *Canadian Wildlife Service Report Series* 5 (1968), page 5.

132:18–33   Vagn Flyger "The Polar Bear: A Matter for International Concern." *Arctic* 20(3) (1967), pages 146 and 153.

BIBLIOGRAPHY

JOURNALS

Baker, B. E., Harington, C. R., and Symes, A. L. "Polar Bear Milk, I. Gross composition and fat constitution." *Canadian Journal of Zoology* 41(6) (1963).

Brooks, J.W. "Infra-red Scanning for Polar Bears." Paper from the Second International Conference on Bear Research and Management. Morges, Switzerland, *International Union for Conservation of Nature and Natural Resources.* (IUCN), (1970).

Cook, R. C. "Gene—The Hybrid Bear." *Journal of Heredity* 41(2) (1950).

Davies, M. "Hybrids of the Polar and Kodiak Bear." *Journal of Mammalogy* 31(4) (1950).

Doutt, J. K. "Toxicity of Polar Bear Liver." *Journal of Mammalogy* 21(3) (1940).

Doutt, J. K. "Polar Bear Dens on the Twin Island, James Bay, Canada." *Journal of Mammalogy* 48(3) (1967).

Fay, F. H. "Experimental transmission of Trichinella spiralis via marine amphipods." *Canadian Journal of Zoology* 46(3) (1968).

Federal Register, Vol. 37, No. 216 (1972).

Flyger, V. "The Polar Bear: A Matter for International Concern." *Arctic* 20(3) (1967).

Flyger, V., and Townsend, M. R. "The Migration of Polar Bears." *Scientific American* 218(2) (1968).

Gavin, A. "Notes on Mammals Observed in the Perry River District Queen Maud Sea." *Journal of Mammalogy* 26(3) (1954).

Harington, C. R. "Denning Habits of the Polar Bear (Ursus maritimus Phipps)." *Canadian Wildlife Service Report Series* 5 (1968).

Hennig, R. "Die Kenntis des Eisbären im Mittelalter." *Zool. Garten* 3(⅓) (1930).

Hock, R. J. "Seasonal Variations in Physiologic Functions of Arctic Ground Squirrels and Black Bears." *Bulletin Museum Comparative Zoology Harvard* 124 (1960).

Jonkel, C. J. "Life History, Ecology and Biology of the Polar Bear, Autumn 1966 Studies." *Progress Notes, Canadian Wildlife Service.* 1 (1967).

Jonkel, C. J. "Polar Bear Research in Canada." *Progress Notes, Canadian Wildlife Service.* 13 (1969).

Jonkel, C. J. "Some Comments on Polar Bear Management." *Biological Conservation* 2(2) (1970).

Jonkel, Kolenosky, Robertson, and Russell. "Further Notes on Polar Bear Denning Habits." Paper from the Second International Conference on Bear Research and Management. Morges, Switzerland, *International Union for Conservation of Nature and Natural Resources.* (IUCN), (1970).

Kistchinski and Uspenski "Immobilization and Tagging of Polar Bears in Maternity Dens." Paper from the Second International Conference on Bear Research and Management. Morges, Switzerland, *International Union for Conservation of Nature and Natural Resources.* (IUCN), (1970).

Klein, D. R. "Problems in Conservation of Mammals in the North." *Biological Conservation* 4(2) (1972).

Kostjan, E. J. "Eisbären und ihr Wachstum." *Zool. Garten* 7(7/9) (1934).

Kurten, B. "The Evolution of the Polar Bear, Ursus maritimus Phipps." *Acta Zoologica Fennica* 108 (1964).

Larsen, T. "Norwegian Polar Bear Hunt, Management and Research." Paper from the Second International Conference on Bear Research and Management. Morges, Switzerland, *International Union for Conservation of Nature and Natural Resources.* (IUCN), (1970).

Larsen, T. "Polar Bear Research in Spitsbergen." *Oryx* 10(6) (1970).

Larsen, T. "Sexual Dimorphism in the Molar Rows of the Polar Bear." *Journal of Wildlife Management* 35(2) (1971).

Larsen, Thor "Polar Bear: Lonely Nomad of the North." *National Geographic* 139(4) (1971).

Lentfer, J. W. "A Technique for Immobilizing and Marking Polar Bears." *Journal of Wildlife Management* 32(2) (1968).

Lentfer, J. W. "Polar Bear—Sea Ice Relationship." Paper from the Second International Conference on Bear Research and Management. Morges, Switzerland, *International Union for Conservation of Nature and Natural Resources.* (IUCN) (1970).

Lewis, H. F. and Doutt, J. K. "Records of the Atlantic Walrus and the Polar Bear in or near the Northern Part of the Gulf of St. Lawrence." *Journal of Mammalogy* 23(4) (1942).

Lewis, R. W. and Lentfer, J. W. "The Vitamin A Content of Polar Bear Liver: Range and Variability." *Comparative Biochemical Physiology* 22(3) (1967).

Oritsland, N. A. "Temperature Regulation of the Polar Bear (Thalartos Maritimus)." *Comparative Biochemistry and Physiology* 37(2) (1970).

Rausch, R., Babero, B. B., Rausch, R. V. and Schiller, E. L. "Studies on the Helminth Fauna of Alaska. XXVII. The Occurrence of Larvae of *Trichinella Spiralis* in Alaskan Mammals." *Journal of Parasitology* 42(3) (1955).

Quay, W. B. "Observations on Mammals of the Seward Peninsula, Alaska." *Journal of Mammalogy* 32(1) (1950).

Schein, M. and Hart, F. M. "A Close Look at Polar Bears." *Animal Kingdom* 65(6) (1962).

Uspenski and Kistchinski "New Data on the Winter Ecology of the Polar Bear on Wrangel Island." Paper from the Second International Conference on Bear Research and Management. Morges, Switzerland, *International Union for Conservation of Nature and Natural Resources.* (IUCN) (1970).

BOOKS

Beechey, Capt. F. W. *A Voyage of Discovery Towards the North Pole.* London: Richard Bentley, 1843.

Conway, Sir Martin *Early Dutch and English Voyages to Spitsbergen in the Seventeenth Century.* London: The Hakluyt Society, 1902.

Crandall, L. S. *The Management of Wild Mammals in Captivity.* Chicago: The University of Chicago Press, 1964.

Gerrit de Veer. *The Three Voyages of William Barents to the Arctic Regions.* London: The Hakluyt Society, 1853.

Haig-Thomas, D. *Tracks in the Snow.* London, New York: The Oxford University Press, 1939.

Hamilton, W. J. *American Mammals—Their Lives, Habits and Economic Relation.* New York: McGraw-Hill Co., 1939.

Illingworth, Frank *Wild Life Beyond the North.* New York: Charles Scribner's Sons, 1952.

Kane, Elisha Kent *Arctic Explorations in the Years 1853, 1854, 1855.* Philadelphia: Childs and Peterson, 1855.

Koldeway, Captain *The German Arctic Expedition of 1869–70.* London: Sampson Low, Marston, Low, and Searle, 1874.

Markham, Albert Hastings. *The Voyages and Works of John Davis.* London: The Hakluyt Society, 1880.

Matthews, L. H. *The Life of Mammals-Vol. I.* London: Weidenfeld and Nicolson, 1969.

M'Clintock, Captain. *The Voyage of the "Fox" in the Arctic Seas. A Narrative of the Discovery of the Fate of Sir John Franklin and His Companions.* Boston: Ticknor and Fields, 1860.

Miller, J. *True Bear Stories.* Chicago: Rand, McNally and Co., 1900.

Montague, Sydney R. *North To Adventure.* New York: Robert M. McBride and Company, 1939.

Muir, John *The Cruise of the Corwin—Journal of the Arctic Expedition of 1881 in Search of De Long and the* Jeannette. Boston: Houghton-Mifflin Company, 1917.

Munn, T. H. "Prairie Trails and Arctic By-ways." London: Hurst Blackett, 1932.

Nansen, F. *Hunting and Adventure in the Arctic.* London: J. M. Dent and Sons Limited. 1925.

Nansen, F. *Farthest North.* New York: Harper and Brothers Publisher, 1897.

Nelson, E. W. *Wild Animals of North America.* Washington: 1930.

Peary, R. E. *Northward over the Great Ice.* New York: Frederick Stokes Company, 1898.

Peary, R. E. *The North Pole.* New York: Frederick Stokes Co., 1910.

Peary, R. E. *Nearest the Pole.* New York: Doubleday, Page & Co., 1907.

Pederson, Alwin *Polar Animals.* New York: Taplinger Publishing Co. Inc., 1966.

Perry, Richard. *The World of the Polar Bear*. Seattle, Washington: University of Washington Press, 1966.

Richardson, Sir John *The Polar Regions*. Edinburgh: Adam and Charles Black, 1861.

Schwatka, F. *Nimrod in the North or Hunting and Fishing Adventures in the Arctic Regions*. New York: Cassell and Company Limited, 1885.

Seton, E. T. *Lives of Game Animals*. New York: Doubleday, Doran and Company, 1929.

Stefansson, V. *Arctic Manual*. New York: The Macmillan Co., 1944.

Stefansson, V. *Hunters of the Great North*. New York: Harcourt, Brace and Company, 1922.

Stefansson, V. *My Life With the Eskimo*. New York: The Macmillan Company, 1924.

Stefansson, V. *Not By Bread Alone*. New York: The Macmillian Co., 1946.

Stefansson, V. *The Friendly Arctic*. New York: The Macmillan Company, 1943.

Stefansson, V. *The Adventures of Wrangel Island*. London: 1926.

Sutton, G. M. *Eskimo Year, A Naturalist's Adventures in the Far North*. New York: The Macmillan Company, 1934.

Thule Expedition (5th) 1921–24. Report #3. Gyldendalske Boghandel, Nordisk Forlag, Copenhagen, 1941.

Tyrrel, J. W. *Across the Sub-Arctic of Canada*. Toronto: William Buggs, 1897.